Subjectivity and Social Change in Higher Education

Social Theory and Methodology in Education Research

Series Editor: Mark Murphy

The Bloomsbury Social Theory and Methodology in Education Research series brings together books exploring various applications of social theory in educational research design. Each book provides a detailed account of how theory and method influence each other in specific educational research settings, such as schools, early childhood education, community education, further education colleges and universities. Books in the series represent the richness of topics explored in theory-driven education research, including leadership and governance, equity, teacher education, assessment, curriculum and policy studies. This innovative series provides a timely platform for highlighting the wealth of international work carried out in the field of social theory and education research, a field that has grown considerably in recent years and has made the likes of Pierre Bourdieu and Michel Foucault familiar names in educational discourse. Books in the Social Theory and Methodology in Education Research series offer an excellent resource for those who wish to use theoretical concepts in their research but are not sure how to do so, and who want to better understand how theory can be effectively applied in research contexts, in practically realisable ways.

Advisory Board:
Julie Allan, University of Birmingham, UK
Robert Aman, University of Glasgow, UK
Stephen Ball, UCL Institute of Education, UK
Cristina Costa, University of Strathclyde, UK
Dympna Devine, University College Dublin, Ireland
Donald Gillies, University of the West of Scotland, UK
Jones Irwin, Dublin City University, Ireland
Bob Lingard, University of Queensland, Australia
Amy Stambach, University of Wisconsin-Madison, USA
Andrew Wilkins, University of East London, UK

Also available in the series:
Foucault and School Leadership Research: Bridging Theory and Method,
Denise Mifsud

Education Governance and Social Theory: Interdisciplinary Approaches to Research, edited by Andrew Wilkins and Antonio Olmedo

International Perspectives on Theorizing Aspirations: Applying Bourdieu's Tools, edited by Garth Stahl, Derron Wallace, Ciaran Burke and Steven Threadgold

Norbert Elias and the Sociology of Education, Eric Lybeck

Post-Qualitative Research and Innovative Methodologies, Matthew K E Thomas and Robin Bellingham

Social Theory and the Politics of Higher Education: Critical Perspectives on Institutional Research, edited by Mark Murphy, Ciaran Burke, Cristina Costa and Rille Raaper

Social Theory for Teacher Education Research: Beyond the Technical-Rational, edited by Kathleen Nolan and Jennifer Tupper

Forthcoming in the series:
Education Research with Bourdieu, Shaun Rawolle

Subjectivity and Social Change in Higher Education

A Collaborative Arts-Based Narrative

Liezl Dick and Marguerite Müller

BLOOMSBURY ACADEMIC
LONDON • NEW YORK • OXFORD • NEW DELHI • SYDNEY

BLOOMSBURY ACADEMIC
Bloomsbury Publishing Plc
50 Bedford Square, London, WC1B 3DP, UK
1385 Broadway, New York, NY 10018, USA
29 Earlsfort Terrace, Dublin 2, Ireland

BLOOMSBURY, BLOOMSBURY ACADEMIC and the Diana logo are trademarks of
Bloomsbury Publishing Plc

First published in Great Britain 2021
This paperback edition published in 2023

Copyright © Liezl Dick and Marguerite Müller, 2021

Liezl Dick and Marguerite Müller have asserted their right under the Copyright,
Designs and Patents Act, 1988, to be identified as Authors of this work.

Series design: Louise Dugdale
Cover image: © Fanatic Studio/Gary Waters/SCIENCE PHOTO LIBRARY

All rights reserved. No part of this publication may be reproduced or transmitted
in any form or by any means, electronic or mechanical, including photocopying,
recording, or any information storage or retrieval system, without prior permission
in writing from the publishers.

Bloomsbury Publishing Plc does not have any control over, or responsibility for, any
third-party websites referred to or in this book. All internet addresses given in this
book were correct at the time of going to press. The author and publisher regret any
inconvenience caused if addresses have changed or sites have ceased to exist, but can
accept no responsibility for any such changes.

A catalogue record for this book is available from the British Library.

Names: Dick, Liezl, author. | Muller, Marguerite, author.
Title: Subjectivity and social change in higher education: a collaborative
arts-based narrative / Liezl Dick and Marguerite Muller.
Description: London; New York, NY: Bloomsbury Academic, 2021. |
Series: Social theory and methodology in education research |
Includes bibliographical references and index. |
Identifiers: LCCN 2021006707 (print) | LCCN 2021006708 (ebook) |
ISBN 9781350123618 (hardback) | ISBN 9781350123625 (ebook) |
ISBN 9781350123632 (epub)
Subjects: LCSH: Educational sociology–South Africa. | Education,
HIgher–Social aspects–South Africa. | Social change--South Africa. |
College teachers–South Africa. | Subjectivity.
Classification: LCC LC191.98.S59 D53 2021 (print) |
LCC LC191.98.S59 (ebook) | DDC 306.430968–dc23
LC record available at https://lccn.loc.gov/2021006707
LC ebook record available at https://lccn.loc.gov/2021006708

ISBN: HB: 978-1-3501-2361-8
PB: 978-1-3502-2496-4
ePDF: 978-1-3501-2362-5
eBook: 978-1-3501-2363-2

Series: Social Theory and Methodology in Education Research

Typeset by Newgen KnowledgeWorks Pvt. Ltd., Chennai, India

To find out more about our authors and books visit
www.bloomsbury.com and sign up for our newsletters.

To our families, our colleagues and our students

Contents

List of Figures		x
Series Editor's Foreword, Mark Murphy		xii
1	If You Want to Go Far, Go Together	1
2	Assembling Roots and Writing a Book: Theory and Methodology Meet	19
3	A Tale of the Assembled Subject: Exploring Whiteness	35
4	Finding What You Have Not Yet Lost: An Affective Inquiry into Educator Subjectivity	53
5	To Not Be Unworthy of What Happens to Us, We Go to the Morgues Ourselves: Wounded Becomings	79
6	Can You Please Come Back Later? A Cartography of Becoming Educators	101
7	More than Human: An Exploration of the Entanglement of Educator Subjectivity and Space	123
8	We Are Not Statues: Becoming with Hope and Uncertainty	141
Epilogue		159
Notes		175
References		179
Index		187

Figures

1	Crying twice, c. 2020	1
2	The wound, 2020	9
3	Digging a hole, 2019	20
4	Tea for two, 2019	30
5	Liezl and the rhizome, 2019	32
6	What you cannot control, 2019	33
7	I'm sorry, 2018	38
8	Do you think this is real? 2018	40
9	Growing up in the 1980s, 2018	43
10	Straight lines, 2014	44
11	And then I left, 2018	45
12	What do I make possible? 2019	61
13	Who we are and what we do, 2019	64
14	Liezl is typing, 2020	73
15	A silent march, 2019	80
16	Four women, 2019	87
17	How we got here, 2019	98
18	Analysis drawing, 2019	100
19	Dandelion, 2019	103
20	A map of the UFS campus, 2019	104
21	The line we walked, 2019	127
22	A place that hurts, 2019	128
23	Then and later, 2016 and 2019	130
24	Steve Biko House, 2016 and 2019	131
25	A dot on the line, 2019	132
26	*Thinking Stone*, 2011	133
27	Barbed wire, 2019	135
28	Cartesian subject? 2019	136
29	A new wall, 2019	138
30	Video chat meeting	146
31	Drinking tea during a pandemic, 2019	160
32	Corona virus is here, 2019	163

33	Force majeure, 2020	168
34	And when the journey ends, 2020	170
35	We laugh, 2020	174

Series Editor's Foreword
Mark Murphy

Education research has a long history of adapting ideas from social theory. While this has always been the case when it comes to educational foundations, in recent years there has been an enormous growth in the adoption of social theory in the field of educational research. The names of theorists such as Pierre Bourdieu, Jürgen Habermas, Judith Butler and Michel Foucault have become commonplace in the field, making social theory evermore familiar to those who both conduct education research and utilise it in their teaching.

As its familiarity increases, so too does the desire to engage with social theory in more thoughtful and effective ways. There is currently a pressing desire to apply social theory in educational research contexts, which makes sense, as without theory, much education research can be overly descriptive and/or restricted by narrow definitions of professional practice. Social theory can assist in efforts to transcend the everyday taken-for-granted understandings of education, while also reflecting erstwhile concerns around power, control, social justice and transformation.

The issue then becomes one of applying theory to method, with the focus shifting to a growing interest in the art of application itself. This interest comes with a set of key questions attached:

- How best to apply concepts such as habitus, subjectivation and performativity in educational research contexts?
- What are the ways in which methodological concerns meet theoretical ones?
- In what ways does social theory shape the quality of research outcomes?

These questions require thoughtful responses, and the purpose of this book series is to help provide solutions to these issues, while also helping to develop the capacity, in particular of postgraduate and early career researchers, to successfully put social theory to work in research. This is especially important as theory application in method is a challenging and daunting enterprise. The set of theories developed by the likes of Foucault, Derrida, Bourdieu et al. could never be described as 'simple' or easy to navigate. On top of that there are a variety of issues faced when applying such ideas in research contexts, a field of complex interwoven imperatives and practices in its own right. These challenges – epistemological, operational, analytical – inevitably impact on researchers and our attempts to make sense of research questions, whether these be questions of governance and political regulation, social reproduction, power, cultural or professional identities (among others). So care needs to be taken when applying a challenging set of ideas onto a challenging set of practices, incorporating a consideration for both intellectual arguments alongside the concerns of the professional researcher.

The series should hold a strong appeal to researchers who are keen to apply social theory in their research, as evidenced by the growing audience for the editor's own website www.socialtheoryapplied.com. It will offer an excellent resource for those who wish to begin using theoretical concepts in their research and will also appeal to readers who have an interest in better understanding how theory can be effectively applied in research contexts, in practically realisable ways.

In terms of output, this series is designed to provide a collection of books exploring various applications of social theory in educational research design. Each book provides a detailed account of how theory and method influence each other in specific educational research settings, such as schools, early years, community education, further education colleges and universities. The series represents the richness of topics explored in theory-driven education research, including leadership and governance, equity, teacher education, assessment, curriculum and policy studies. It also provides a timely platform for highlighting the wealth of work done in the field of social theory and education research, a field that has grown considerably in recent years and has made the likes of Pierre Bourdieu and Michel Foucault familiar names in educational discourse.

Embedded in the design of the series is an explicit pedagogical component, with a focus on the 'how' of applying theory in research methodology and an emphasis on operationalising theory in research. This pedagogical remit is addressed explicitly in the texts in different ways – the responsibility of addressing this falls to the authors and editors, but can take the form of case studies, learning activities, 'focus' sections and glossaries detailing the key theoretical concepts utilised in the research.

The current book, *Subjectivity and Social Change in Higher Education: A Collaborative Arts-Based Narrative*, co-authored by Liezl Dick and Marguerite Müller, is a strong addition to the book series. The book adapts the ideas of

Gilles Deleuze and Félix Guattari and puts them to work in exploring the field of educator professional identity. It is a collaborative text developed from the shared experiences and scholarly work of the authors, building on their time working in student residences at the University of the Free State, South Africa. This context sees educator identities being confronted by widespread student protests (#fallist movements) at South African universities and a call for rapid transformation, inclusivity and decolonisation. The text is a response to this call – as the authors put it, the book aims 'to use theory and methodology to create new and authentic ways of thinking about professional educator subjectivity in relation to rapid social change' (Marguerite and Liezl, *Subjectivity and Social Change*, p. 71).

Both the theoretical approach and the specific area of investigation are increasingly popular in theory-driven forms of education research, and as a result I envisage a strong readership for this text. The book offers readers an important vantage point from which to understand and engage with the specific form of post-structuralist thought as applied to educational research. It offers an excellent resource in particular for those who wish to research issues of educator identity via innovative methodological approaches, including post-qualitative, arts-based, autobiographical, ethnographic and collaborative methods of inquiry. I am very pleased that the authors have adopted the spirit of the overall book series – strong links are made throughout between theory and method in education research. It is written in an accessible style and the stylistic approach (conversational, author-biographical, dramaturgical) is pedagogically innovative as well as appropriate for the readership. Many thanks to Liezl and Marguerite for making such a strong contribution to the series and to the broader field of theory-driven education research.

1

If You Want to Go Far, Go Together

Figure 1 Crying twice, c. 2020.
Photograph courtesy Katinka de Wet.

1.1 The Snapshot

There is a saying that Bloemfontein will make you cry twice: once when you arrive and once when you leave. Bloemfontein lies in the heart of the Free State, in the middle of South Africa. Our story unfolds against this backdrop, of blue skies and pale yellow grasslands that stretch out as far as the eye can see. We both arrived here from different places. Our paths crossed here. The crossing and connection made something possible. A collaboration. A book. A story to tell.

This book is a snapshot of educator experiences during a time of rapid change in South African higher education. Our writing collaboration started in 2015 and still continues today, in 2020, when the impact of student movements,[1] such as #RhodesMustFall and #FeesMustFall, brought about rapid change in our context. Our exploration of educator subjectivity and social change is located in our specific postcolonial, post-apartheid context, where calls for decolonization have intensified in recent years. However, our story should also be seen against a global backdrop, where movements such as #BlackLivesMatter and the impact of COVID-19 continue to change how we think about social change, education and educator subjectivity.

There is no beginning or end to this story; it is merely a rhizomatic adventure we undertook, which gives you, the reader, a glimpse into a moment in the lives of educators in a specific place at a specific time: '[the rhizomatic] know how to move between things, establish a logic of the AND, overthrow ontology, do away with foundations, nullify endings and beginnings' (Deleuze 2004a, xiv–xv; Williams 2013, 126–7). Our perspective is shaped by a snapshot: it is like driving through the Free State and leaning out of the car window to take pictures of the landscape with your phone. The picture shows you something of the landscape but does not show you everything. You could always take a different picture, from a different angle or at a different time of day on a different part of your journey. So, what we offer here is a snapshot, taken by us, from a certain place at a certain time. It is no more and no less than that.

1.2 The Journey

There is an African proverb that advises, if you want to go fast, go alone; if you want to go far, go together. In writing this book, we embarked on a journey, together, to explore the complexity of educator identity and social change. Our collaboration formed when our paths crossed, not for the first time, at the University of the Free State (UFS), where we both worked as campus residence managers and were studying towards doctorates in higher education. Informed by our PhD studies and lived experiences, we started to think about how our personal experiences in this context were shaping our professional identities. Our exploration resulted in this book, in which we dwell upon educator subjectivity as it unfolds in a landscape of social change in the South African higher education context. As we were together on his journey, we were looking at the same landscape, which, to each of us looked different through a different window. Because we saw different angles of the same view, we wanted to explore what these different perspectives and approaches could make possible. The collaborative work that emerged from our shared experiences made it possible to explore education research as a creative engagement, which blurred the lines between our personal and professional lives.

1.3 Educator Subjectivity and Social Change

Our interest in educator subjectivity and social change is informed by the rapidly changing higher education environment in South Africa. However, our local, contextual understandings must be framed by the bigger global context. In 2020, we saw major shifts happening around the world. The COVID-19 pandemic spread from country to country, leading to national lockdowns, and work from home became the new norm. Education swiftly moved from physical classroom spaces to virtual and digital platforms. Suddenly, teachers around the world were teaching from their living rooms. A sudden move out of the traditional workplace setting into the personal space undoubtedly influences the way we think about professional identity. Although this book is not about the impact of COVID-19 on the lives of educators, it does touch on the professional and personal shifts that happened in our lives due to this new reality.

The COVID-19 pandemic also exposed some of the fault lines and inequalities in the South African education landscape further (Schreiber, Moja and Luescher 2020). South African campuses, which had resources and infrastructure in place, were left deserted as students returned to their homes, where vastly different realities awaited. For some students, the transition from face-to-face to online learning was a seamless process that was supported by technology and secure internet connections being available. For most of them, however, returning home meant returning to informal and rural settlements where technological devices are hard to come by and the internet connection is unstable and often unavailable.

The year 2020 also saw worldwide protest movements in the wake of the police murder of George Floyd, on 25 May in Minneapolis, in the United States. The #BlackLivesMatter movement and protests gained support and momentum across the globe. 'Floyd's slow eight-minute asphyxiation, captured on video by a passer-by, prompted passionate protests across the world and added fresh urgency to campaigns demanding the removal of statues that glorify figures whose reputations (and fortunes) were built on crushing peoples of colour and the stifling of indigenous cultures' (BBC News 2020).

Statues that were toppled included that of the eighteenth-century British slave trader Edward Colston, in Bristol, England, as well as those of Confederate president Jefferson Davis and Christopher Columbus, in the United States. Thousands of people gathered in Oxford to demand the removal of a statue of 'Cecil Rhodes, a British supremacist who enriched himself by exploiting Africa's people and resources' (BBC News 2020). All of this happened almost five years after Rhodes's statue had been removed from the campus of the University of Cape Town during the #RhodesMustFall protests. Thus, when we talk of the context of rapid social change and transformation, we are speaking from a South African angle, but not about an exclusively South African phenomenon.

In this book, we situate our exploration of educator subjectivity as emerging in response to events that bring about sudden change, such as student protests, and COVID-19. Readers should note that, in our understanding, the term educator is not restricted to formal academic or teaching staff but also encompasses support staff and student leadership, as people who enter into pedagogical relationships with students. Many of the educators who participated in our research on educator subjectivity were employed in the UFS Division of Student Affairs, where they held positions that support students and manage residence spaces. Furthermore, many staff members who hold positions as residence managers also teach or study at the university. Because residence managers live on campus, they are often exposed to social and academic projects of the university, which provide them with experiences that bridge a personal/professional binary. This continuum enables residence mangers to have a transversal perspective (Guattari 2015) of the processes of subjectification that play out in the university space.

In our roles as educators, residence managers, students and academics we experience many changes and flows that continuously weave through the fibre of higher education, though not all with the same intensity or speed. In light of this changing context, it is imperative to contemplate subjectivities that differ from those shaped by colonial powers, hierarchical, patriarchal and racialized institutions and, most of all, our thinking habits. This changing context requires us, as educators and researchers, to *be* different, *think* differently, and *do* things differently (Müller 2018). We, hence, explore a rhizomatic notion of subjectivity that is affective, processual and always in flux, rather than fixed and static. Our thinking around subjectivity as an emergent and responsive force is informed by the Deleuzoguattarian concepts of assemblage and the wound-event (these concepts are discussed in Sections 1.4.1 and 1.4.2).

1.4 Where Are We Going, and What Will Help Us Get There?

The aim of this book was to use theory and methodology to create new and authentic ways of thinking about professional educator subjectivity in relation to rapid social change. We explore the concept of educator subjectivity by conceptualizing it along a personal/professional continuum. Educator subjectivity is viewed as an entangled expression of professional and personal experience in the education context. We explore this non-binary understanding of subjectivity through a conflation of theory and methodology. A Deleuzoguattarian ontology, which views subjectivity as assembled, and which disrupts a traditional professional/personal educator identity description, is in line with a narrative tradition in education research that focuses on educator identity and experience, as key elements in shaping education contexts and change.

By working with a professional/personal educator identity continuum, rather than the professional and the personal as binary oppositions, we indicate our interest in examining the way this continuum helps us to move towards social change, transformation and decolonization. As such, we employ a Deleuzoguattarian lens, which brings the assembled subject into focus and makes it possible for us to explore the performance of subjectivity through micro-social occurrences and affective becomings. This book is, thus, theoretically embedded in the work of Deleuze and Guattari, with a specific focus on Deleuze's ontology of difference and his critique of the traditional image of thought, and dogmatic and common-sense thinking habits. Deleuze (2004a) criticizes Western philosophy's obsession with identity in thought, by claiming that the traditional image of thought upholds a notion of difference that is merely conceptual and does not explore difference-in-itself, which Deleuze also understands as becoming. A dogmatic image of thought stifles our ability to think, which limits, by implication, our becoming(s) in this world. In *Difference and Repetition,* Deleuze (2004a) provides a thorough critique of this traditional image of thought, and in *A Thousand Plateaus,* Deleuze, together with Guattari (2008), provides an alternative to the arboreal image of thought. With the help of figurations, such as the rhizome, assemblage, cartography and the fold, Deleuze and Gauttari make it possible for us to think beyond binaries, towards multiplicities, as they explore what it means to think about difference-in-itself, that is, becoming. Their vegetal image of thought makes it possible to think differently about subjectivity, thought and becoming/being, and to explore the affective 'foundations' of an alternative image of thought. Subjectivity is the processual product of an affective assemblage, where the subject also forms part of a non-heterogeneous assemblage that consists of human and non-human elements. Such an ontology of subjectivity has far-reaching epistemological and methodological effects, considering that the processual 'production' of subjectivity affects the way the subject knows and is known. Deleuze and Guattari's assembled understanding of subjectivity can help us to think differently about educator subjectivity and knowledge production in the higher education space. In light of calls for decolonization, and a rapidly changing COVID-19 context, educators are obliged to question existing notions of educator subjectivity. Processes of subjectification, dominated by colonial flows of power, patriarchal domination and polarized and categorical thinking habits, do not hold anymore. To adapt to our rapidly changing working and living environments, we have to think differently, and authentically, about personal and professional subjectivities, and how they relate to each another. Therefore, the theoretical position we embraced enabled us to explore the educator identity continuum as expressions of being, belonging and becoming, through which transformative possibilities emerge in educational contexts. The guiding question for our book is, how can we use theory and methodology to think differently about educator subjectivity during a time of rapid change? To think 'differently' implies a critical, novel, creative and authentic engagement with our own subjectivities, and those we are relationally co-created and co-creating with.

We use arts-based inquiry as an overarching term that encompasses narrative, performative and autobiographical methods of inquiry. Our self-reflective style enables us to embrace 'the constant processualism of practice' while writing and living towards a 'future [that] is never fixed and always lives within the unexpected notyetness of each new encounter' (Gale 2020, 304).

In this book, we wanted to keep the dynamism of living though transformative times alive. Central to our collaboration are notions of experimentation, creation and exploration. We do not merely want to tell you the stories of educators living through transformation; we also want to explore what their narratives make possible. Similarly, we were curious to find out what the theory and concepts we use can make possible. We plugged the theory and concepts into our own lives and the narratives of our participants – the place and space of UFS – because we were curious to see what happens in this research assemblage. 'These theorizings as practice and concept making as event', Gale (2020, 305) writes:

> involve autoethnographers in moving toward practices that are less interpretive, judgmental, and representational and, therefore, toward those that are more creative, speculative, and experimental'. (Gale 2020, 306)

And this is exactly what we are interested in. We are less interested in what concepts mean, and more interested in what they can actually do:

'The question is not: is it true? But: does it work?' (Deleuze and Guattari 2008, xv).

On this journey, we were supported by employing the concepts of the assembled subject and the wound event.

1.4.1 The Assembled Subject

We found that working with the Deleuzoguattarian concepts of assemblage, rhizome and affect, and Deleuze's philosophy of the event, helped us to think differently about educator subjectivity and knowledge production in the higher education space. The theoretical position, which will serve as a backdrop for our research, and which will extend into and connect with the research methodology, enabled us to explore the educator identity continuum as expressions of being, belonging and becoming, through which transformative possibilities emerge in educational contexts. During the writing process, we engaged with several authors and practitioners who work with Deleuze and Guattari's theory. We were, thus, open for a rhizomatic and affective collaboration to come into existence with authors or theoretical and methodological perspectives that resonate with a Deleuzoguattarian notion of affective becoming.

For the purpose of this book, we discern between identity and subjectivity as concepts with different meanings but which are not completely unrelated. Identity can be defined as the product of social conventions – a fiscal necessity generated by the nation-state to execute power and regulate populations. The term identity also reminds us of the cognitive, rational Cartesian subject, whose identity is fixed, insular, timeless and constant. We will engage critically with identity, to move towards structures of subjectivity, where the latter is understood as the affective becoming-other in entangled relationships with human and non-human others. Our aim is to deterritorialize identity as confined within the existing structures of power, in order to explore new ways of being and becoming; in other words, new subjectivities. We consider transformation and change to be becomings – becoming is what happens when affective, rhizomatic connections are made in heterogenous assemblages. Such an understanding of subjectivity will enable us to think and perform our relationality, where this relationality does not only make a novel ontological understanding of subjectivity possible but also enables more ethical, relational and connected subjectivities (Braidotti 2011a).

We are interested in the ways Deleuzoguattarian theory could enable us to trouble Cartesian subjectivity, which might manifest as fixed or essentialized expressions of professional identity. In using the Deleuzoguattarian concept of assemblage, we employ a variety of methodological perspectives that position the subject as emergent, multiple, affective and always becoming-other. Our work is situated in critical, narrative, autobiographical, ethnographic, performative, collaborative and arts-based research traditions, which extend into post-qualitative inquiry. With this multi-method exploration of educator experience and memory, we wish to explore micro-social expressions that serve to reflect larger narratives of social change and transformation. We aim to work against a theory/method binary of traditional qualitative research, and to set the stage for educator subjectivity to emerge as fluid, multiple and responsive. Thus, we will explore how Deleuze and Guattari's alternative assembled and processual understanding of subjectification can help us to engage in a post-qualitative inquiry of educator subjectivity in the higher education space. We perceive subjectivity to be something that is spatio-temporally constituted. The concept of the assemblage will help us to think about (among others things) the spatial dimension of subjectivity; if the subject is relationally constituted in space–time, we have to enquire into the terms of construction of relations. Highlighting the power dynamics in processes of subjectification is, thus, important (Massey 2005, 142).

In light of calls for decolonization, it is imperative to trouble normative and conventional notions of educator subjectivity and to contemplate how different and authentic subjectivities could help educators work to achieve social change and transformation.

1.4.2 The Wound-Event

> One reason for drawing such distinction [between Aion and Chronos] emerges when we consider the paradoxes involved in identifying, in historical time, the precise moment at which events occur. Suppose we take a time before the event and a time after: the infinite divisibility of the series of moments implies that there are two converging series on either side of the event, but no point at which these series meet. Thus, from the perspective of historical time, the event is 'eternally that which has just happened or that which is about to happen'. Another reason for regarding event time as another kind of time or another dimension within

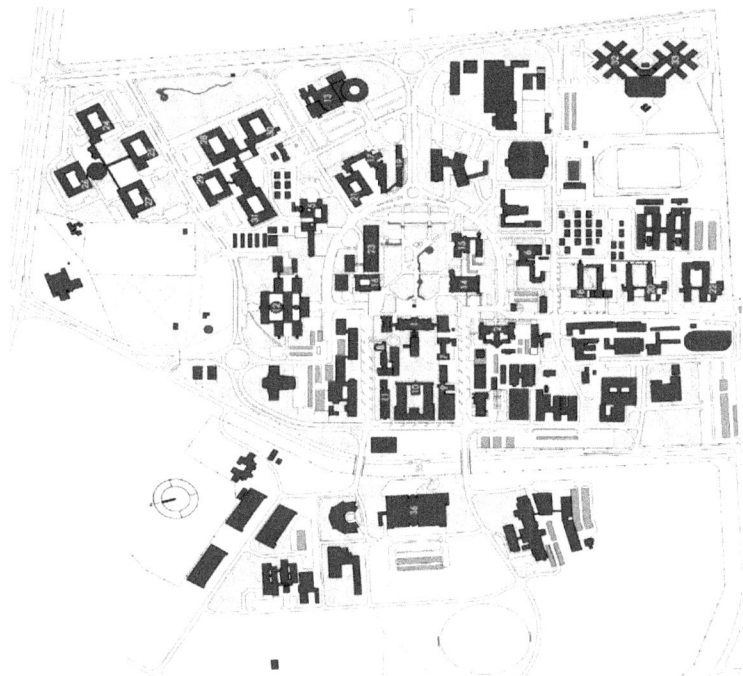

Figure 2 The wound, 2020.

time emerges when we consider the internal structure and complexity of events. Events are complex in the sense that they are always composed of other events, however minimal or momentary. They are structured both internally and by their relations to other events. They often involve long periods when it appears that nothing is happening, and then suddenly everything changes and nothing is the same as before. In this manner, a political regime may collapse or an epoch draw to a close. (Patton 1997, 8)

What will happen if we think differently about who we are, as educators, and who, what and how we are becoming in relation to different understandings of time? If we postulate that who I am depends on who I am becoming, and who I am becoming depends on who I am unbecoming, what does this understanding of the interrelatedness of subjectivity, change and time make possible? In rethinking educator subjectivity, we, the authors, are using ourselves as experimental laboratories. We are actively troubling our 'known', seemingly essentialized subjectivities to embrace growth, movement and rhizomatic connection. In line with an affective, processual and connected understanding of subjectivity, the question, who are you? should rather be, who are you *now*?, or, who are you *becoming*?, or, who are you *unbecoming*?, or even, *with whom* or *what* are you becoming, *when*? By adding timely, processual and relational dimensions to the question of being, it becomes possible to change our thinking habits, from being static, individual and essentialized, towards a becoming-together in space and time and with matter. Hence, we move away from subjectivity, as static and frozen in time, towards a fluid and relational conception of subjectification. Deleuze's concept of the event makes it possible to trouble and rethink the interrelatedness of subjectivity, time and becoming. The event can be described as

> instantaneous productions intrinsic to interactions between various kinds of forces. Events are changes immanent to a confluence of parts or elements, subsisting as pure virtualities (that is, real inherent possibilities) and distinguishing themselves only in the course of their actualisation in some body or state … an event is the potential immanent within a particular confluence of forces. (Stagoll 2010, 89–90)

To understand the value of the notion of the event for our exploration of educator subjectivity, it is important to highlight this connection between subjectivity, time and becoming. Deleuze criticizes a common-sense thinking of time and temporality. He discerns between chronos – chronological, historical and linear time that is 'composed of a series of interlocking presents' (Reynolds 2007, 55) – and the time of the event, Aion – unlimited, incorporeal and empty form of time, 'which subdivides endlessly into the past and future, and the event that likewise never actually occurs in present time' (Reynolds 2007, 55). Aion is associated with surface, wound, event and the virtual, and chronos relates to depth, scar, state of affairs and the actual. The virtual is a creative, transformative and productive sphere, while the actual is the created, the produced, the realm of identities, sameness and all that currently exists. Chronos (the actual) is thus associated with common sense and habit, while Aion (the virtual) is associated with potential, a transcendental field of differences. To understand Deleuze's use of the wound-event, it is important to understand the paradoxical relation between Aion and Chronos. These temporalities seem like opposites, but they are rather interrelated: the one needs the other, and both are incomplete without one other. A process of becoming takes place between these two forms of time, where 'time and space is involved in the paradoxical constitution of sense' (Reynolds 2007, 54).

By working with different notions of time, the event makes it possible to explore 'an inner complexity that is often imperceptible from the point of view of ordinary time, in other words it enables us to make sense of the internal structure of complexity of events' (Patton 2006, 120). Deleuze's philosophy of the event makes it possible to attend to the chronological narratives of educators, while simultaneously reading these stories against the 'backdrop' of colonization and apartheid – events that started long before its occurrence on a linear historical timeline, and with consequences that will outlive our great-grandchildren. Events, in other words, will continue to haunt us. To acknowledge the complexity of narratives and its entanglement with 'empty time', with Aion, is an ethical move, not only not to oversimplify matters but also to provide narratives and their narrators with the opportunity to be worthy of what happens to them. What do we mean by this? By telling their stories, narrators get the opportunity to counter-actualize the wound-event, to come to terms with what happened to them and, most of all, communicate and share these lived experiences: 'if we are connected it is not as identities or through identities. So we do not connect through who we are or what we do, but through how we express the ideas and sense connecting us' (Williams 2008, 170).

Deleuze's event and the way it troubles a common-sense notion of causality, however, also equips us with thinking tools for living and thinking through times of uncertainty. The notion of the event implies that the future influences the present and the past. The implication of this is that how we think and live *now*, determines who and what the world is *becoming*. Deleuze's philosophy of the event hence 'provides new means of description of the forces which shape our future and therefore new possibilities for action' (Patton 1997, 11). Our understanding of reconciliation, equality, justice, fairness and what it means to be a humane human being, for example, impacts our legal, political and economic decision-making processes directly (Patton 1997). Who we are becoming as educators, needless to say, will, thus, determine who our students will become, whose becomings will, in turn, affect the becomings of their students and learners. It is, thus, crucial to interrogate educator subjectivities. To a certain extent, the counter-actualization Deleuze writes about is what we are trying to do to make sense of our changing lives in a time of rapid social change; negotiating the past, imagining the future, doing the writing itself in the present moment, and the being and becoming in another time, which is not chronological or linear. To write, for us, the authors, involves making rhizomatic connections, to become and unbecome and to share. To write is to counter-actualize, to make sense of our past experiences, and to use them to create better futures, not only for ourselves, but for others, too. Subjectivity is relational, our acts and events are intertwined. While writing, we constantly delve into memories to make sense of experiences, while also projecting certain expectations about the future, during a time of acute uncertainty.

When we initially started planning this book, Deleuze's philosophy of the event was not the main aspect of his work that we considered featuring in our project about educator subjectivity and social change. However, COVID-19 not only changed the way we experience the world and how we think about ourselves and others, it also forced its way into our book and demanded a slightly different theoretical focus. What we experienced during 2020, as a year of displacement, disruption, loss, wounding and paradox, called for conceptual thinking tools that could help us to come to terms with the loss of the illusions of stability, predictability, identity, fixity and all other seemingly stable constants. Deleuze's philosophy of the event provided us with the necessary thinking and affective tools to, at least, try to live through the complexity of our times and to guide some sort of becoming-with, flow, flux and continuous transformation. To resist what is happening to us during these pandemic times would result in a stifling of becoming, becoming-other and becoming-with-the-world, and this would only hurt us further. Accepting and working-with the accidents and incidents that befall us, Deleuze (1990) claims, is the way to go if we want to live an affirmative, life-embracing existence of beauty. The only way out is through.

This book will thus take on the form of an event itself. Our lives (the lives of Liezl and Marguerite) are, in turn, events that are entangled with the lives and events of several other educators. The philosophy of the event allows us to play with a different understanding of cause and effect, 'to be punished before having committed a fault, to cry before having pricked oneself, to serve before having divided up the servings' (Deleuze 1990, 3), as well as providing a different idea of how we understand time itself (Reynolds 2007, 53). This approach might seem very abstract, however, the way we think about causality, time and the relation between past, present and future, influences our subjectivities, and educator subjectivity, in particular, which will be the focus of this book. These are insights and awarenesses that we, as post-apartheid South Africans, had been grappling with for a few decades. More recent calls for decolonization, the #fallist movements of the past few years and the need for institutional transformation, confronted the third-world scholar and educator with the need for deep and sustainable personal reflection; the habitual, normal and (mostly) unconscious ways of doing, being and becoming had to be questioned, because that is what the changing times and environment of our country demanded of us. No easy endeavour but crucial and unavoidable. There is no point in resisting change, rather work with and transform with the change. But how do we do this, especially in a deeply traumatized place like South Africa, where the woundedness has been running so deep for so long?

The idea of the wound-event is also particularly helpful for thinking through events such as colonization, apartheid and even the event of COVID-19, as 'temporal wounds'. Instead of thinking (only) spatially about the wound and wounding, Deleuze introduces a notion of the wound-event as an effect and not as a cause. By troubling 'exclusively unidirectional, empiricist understandings of causality' (Reynolds 2007, 53), Deleuze introduces a ghostly, haunting notion of causality that operates at the level of the virtual, and which, as 'quasi-cause', to a certain extent produces the actual. In this sense, the event is never what is happening now, in the present moment; instead, the event 'produces and conditions that which does come about' (Reynolds 2007, 53, 58). This insight is helpful when we have to contemplate the past, the present and the future of events such as apartheid and, possibly, COVID-19, because we can gain insight into the intensities, forces and flows that determine the future, which, consequently, makes it possible for us to contemplate new possibilities of action (Patton 1997, 11). This is possibly brought about by sense, which can be described as the 'increase or decrease of intensity ... the choking of the flow of water, the stifling of trade and the accompanying amplification of misery as a once great city slowly dies. The sense of such events lies ... in the changing flows that invest them with value (Williams 2008, 8).

The changes we are currently experiencing during the time of a pandemic, whether behavioural, psychological, political or social, are an example of the complex relations of sense and a wound-event. A multitude of processes are currently taking place due to COVID-19 and, in this way, the event makes an impact (Williams 2008, 2).

Consequently, we can ask what happens to institutions (such as universities, governments, health systems), subjectivities, towns, neighbourhoods and families when an event resonates through them? What happens to processes of subjectification? The answer is 'They transform themselves with the event that has selected them' (Williams 2008, 2). Educators have no choice but to transform with changing COVID-19 times, with calls for decolonization, towards becoming-other and becoming-different. Who, what and how we are becoming is still undetermined. From the perspective of the 'old order', pre-COVID-19, everything seems to be descending into chaos – an unbecoming and deterritorialization of sorts. From the perspective of futurity, a new order is coming into existence, with new becomings, new ways of being and, possibly, different and more authentic educator subjectivities.

In this book we do not shy away from contradictions and paradoxes; instead, we playfully embrace uncertainties and unpredictability, to avoid being overwhelmed by the unknown and, instead, to embark on a journey initiated by curiosity and becoming into the unknown, carefully excited to see what is to be found. We perceive transformation as becoming, and becoming is viewed as the making of experimental affective connections. What do different notions of time and space make possible for the becomings of educator subjectivities? This is what we will explore in the following chapters. By thinking differently about time (viewing it as non-linear, paradoxical and open to the future) and space (as open, relational, multiple and negotiated), new ways of thinking about subjectivity, and the processes and flows producing subjectivities, become possible.

Scientific writing can remove the dynamism of real life. With this book, we wanted to create ways of bringing this dynamism back by demonstrating and playing with different notions of space and time in the writing of narratives (Massey 2005, 25). The concept of the assemblage will guide our exploration of educator subjectivity in terms of spatiality, while the concept of the wound-event will push our thinking beyond common-sense notions of time. In rethinking educator subjectivity in times of rapid social change, it is important to avoid thinking of time and space as binaries and to think of them as located on a continuum instead; the way we think about space will influence how we think about time and vice versa (Massey 2005, 18). This way of thinking also informed the way the chapters unfolded, as we will explain in the next section.

1.5 Our Route and the Stops We Made on the Way

Our journey together took us to different places and spaces. As we explored the different concepts, such as assemblage, multiplicity, affect, rhizome, becoming and cartography, we had conversations, wrote stories, drank tea and wrote, together. In the following, we outline the focus of each chapter we encountered on the way.

In Chapter 2, 'Assembling Roots and Writing a Book: Theory and Methodology Meet', we will use dialogue to sketch our collaborative process of working, thinking and writing together. The dialogues serve as a tool to unpack the theoretical and methodological angles of this book, and we will explain how this tool might contribute to a project related to decolonization of higher education. We will provide an in-depth discussion of the concepts we used to think about the importance of educator subjectivity in the context of social change, transformation and decolonization. An affective processual subjectivity will be the point of entry for Deleuzoguattarian figurations of assemblage, affect, rhizome, becoming and the use of cartography. We will discuss the literature that provides the theoretical underpinning for these concepts, to inform a narrative that is arts-based, and a post-qualitative inquiry into education research. In Chapter 2, we will initiate a discussion of how theory and methodology might shape research into educator subjectivity and social change in higher education.

In Chapter 3, 'A Tale of the Assembled Subject: Exploring Whiteness', we will take a look at our own assembled subjectivities. We used visual storyboarding to write this chapter as a performative narrative. We will create a non-linear narrative of the way our multiple educator identities unfold against the backdrop of personal and professional experiences. We 'perform' subjectivity as a multiplicity, and explore its affective connections by using a lens of whiteness to unpack our positionality in the context. By positioning whiteness as one aspect of the assembled subject, we seek to understand and trouble essentialized identities and think of subjectivity as multiple and emergent. The purpose and relevance of this chapter are that it serves as a blueprint for research that explores how the personal informs the professional and vice versa. The chapter will conclude with a suggestion for using storyboarding and performative writing in research on educator subjectivity.

In Chapter 4, 'Finding What You Have Not Yet Lost: An Affective Inquiry into Educator Subjectivity', we will explore how arts-based research can make affective connections possible. In this chapter, we will expand our understanding of educator subjectivity by using arts-based research inquiry. We invite educators to reflect on critical incidents and create a collaborative narrative as they make affective connections between these incidents. The affective incidents become points of entry into educators' understanding of the self and other. By using affect as an entry point into subjectivity we open up the possibility for multiple aspects of identity to emerge and conflate as we engage with expression of identity. The chapter demonstrates how the theory and methodology we employ make it possible to conceptualize educator identity as a multiplicity. Through the use of affect we hope to demonstrate the possibilities of a personal/professional educator identity continuum in education for social change.

Chapter 5, 'To Not Be Unworthy of What Happens to Us, We Go to the Morgues Ourselves: Wounded Becomings', will take the shape of a collective biography that explores the rhizomatic, nonlinear and paradoxical becoming of four women. We will present a collective biography of women that explores and interrogates the wound-event as becoming. In this chapter, we will use Deleuze's philosophy of the wound-event to understand subjectivity, as expressed through memory, as an assembled and affective 'event', rather than a fixed entity. The visual autobiographical narratives of educators are created in response to the question, who are we now and how did we get here? In this way, we seek to collaboratively make connections between our experiences and the experiences of others, resulting in a memory assemblage. Through the memory assemblage, we seek to visually explore subjectivity as a multiplicity. Memory has the potential to form a positive feedback loop into professional praxis, which helps us to explore the personal/professional continuum. Here, our arts-based inquiry connects with the act of counter-actualization, to explore the becomings of educators.

The title of Chapter 6 is 'Can You Please Come Back Later? A Cartography of Becoming Educators'. In this chapter, we use non-linear time to play with the idea of becoming educators. We specifically employed the narratives of students who had become educators during a time of rapid social change in higher education in South Africa. By conflating the personal/professional educator identity binary, we hope to show ways of thinking creatively through social change and transformation. The chapter uses cartography to plug and connect narratives into each other. This entangled expression of becoming will show how educator subjectivity develops through disruption and encounter. This process is non-linear and non-causal and highlights the value of moving away from common-sense notions of time and space.

In Chapter 7, 'More than Human: An Exploration of the Entanglement of Educator Subjectivity and Space', we turn to more-than-human subjectivity to explore how refrains and lines shape our embeddedness in place. In keeping with the theoretical underpinnings presented in the preceding chapters, place will be conceptualized as assembled and affective and consisting of networks of human and non-human actors that continuously become-other as they come into relation with one another. It is envisioned that exploring these relations, and the becomings they produce, will provide openings to critically consider personal/professional educator identity in terms of its materiality as it finds expression within a specific place. We aim to show how walking as transformative pedagogy can help us to consider the material and affective aspects of the recent calls for transformation, social change and decolonization at higher education institutions in South Africa.

Chapter 8,' We Are Not Statues: Becoming with Hope and Uncertainty', serves as the conclusion this book. This chapter is a reflective exercise, in which we use our research assemblage to demonstrate that the educator identity is multiple, diverse and creative. Our thesis is that an educator identity that is understood as nomadic, assembled and affective can create new possibilities for professional identity in a time of rapid social change. We will refer to Chapters 2, 3, 4 and 5 to draw connections and theorize a new vision for educator identity and making new rhizomatic becomings possible. We will also demonstrate how the different chapters form a research assemblage. This chapter is a reflective exercise on what theory and methodology made possible for our research on educator subjectivity. We will reflect on how different chapters form a research assemblage. The explorations in previous chapters lead us to think about how hope and uncertainty informed the becoming of educators during a time of rapid social change.

The epilogue is a background sketch of the processes of thinking and engagement that are needed for a collaborative writing project. We think of it in terms of the 'negative' of the photo or the snapshot, the behind-the-scene or as the reserve of the drawing (Ingold 2010). The epilogue unfolds as a timeline of reflective responses to our experiences of writing this book and how those experiences allowed us to think about educator subjectivity and the changing higher education context.

1.6 Chasing the Horizon

Our collaboration in writing this book developed from shared experiences and scholarly work within student residences at the UFS and shared research interests. As we lived and worked through the #fallist movements, we began to see a need for alternative ways of knowledge production that might counter hierarchal power dynamics in research. We felt the need to explore more complex ways of knowing and being, which resulted in alternative epistemologies for responding to the complexity of social change, decolonization and social justice in education. By understanding the subject as multiple and emergent, rather than centred and fixed, we hope to open up new research avenues for studies on educator identity. We hope this book will help educators and researchers to explore how professional and personal educator subjectivity exist along a continuum, rather than in binary terms.

Furthermore, the book might help educators to respond in a socially just way to the complexity and diversity of educational contexts amidst rapid social change. We simply offer a snapshot of one context and the experiences of a few people; however, our hope is to create research that takes an affective, performative and aesthetic form that makes scholarly work accessible to academic and non-academic audiences alike.

2

Assembling Roots and Writing a Book: Theory and Methodology Meet

2.1 Construction Site

Liezl and Marguerite meet in a small office on the southern side of the Education Faculty building. They are writing a book. They are writing *this* book. They are writing me.

The office does not get much sun. A large window overlooks an old parking lot that has been partially demolished to make room for a new building project. The persistent beep … beep … beep of the construction vehicles echo against a sunny autumn sky in Bloemfontein. They sit at a little round table, with two laptops, a pile of drawings and notes, coffee cups, a water bottle and a small aloe plant in a unicorn-shaped flowerpot. Liezl takes a sip of coffee as she looks at the digger that is moving dirt around outside. It creates little hills of rubble that seem strangely out of place on the characteristically flat landscape, where the horizon stretches out to the limits of what can be imagined. Marguerite is doodling absent-mindedly on a piece of paper.

Marguerite: How do we go about this? How do we write a book?
Liezl: How do we write it together?

We want to tell a story of our lived experiences as educators at the UFS. In telling the story, we hope to explore educator subjectivity during a time of rapid change. However, we approach this project from two different angles. On the one hand, we want to explore *how* to tell the story, and on the other, we need to understand what the story *makes possible* in terms of our understanding of educator subjectivity. The *how* and the *why* and the *so what* need to come together as we write this book. We want the method and the theory to function on a continuum, rather than stand separately from each other. In doing this,

Figure 3 Digging a hole, 2019.
Pen and highlighter on paper, Marguerite Müller.

we hope to do research that is responsive to our context of rapid change and transformation.

> **Marguerite:** So, we want to bridge the theory/method dichotomy in order to create a new way of thinking about educator subjectivity … to create a kind of toolbox for doing research with educator subjectivity.
> **Book:** I listen to their conversation and realize that they are writing me from two different angles. Liezl is thinking from the angle of theory, and Marguerite is more interested in the method of creation. This is how they come together to write. Each with their specific interest, perspective and point of entry.
> **Liezl:** We come from different angles, but we ask the same question.

Marguerite: How can we use theory and methodology to think differently about educator subjectivity during a time of rapid change?

Liezl: We need experimental theoretical underpinnings and methodological approaches that can help us think beyond fixed binaries and allow the subject to be fluid, emerging and always already becoming. Deleuze and Guattari's concepts form a backdrop for our research, which help us look beyond essentializing identity politics and enable us to engage with educator subjectivity as multiple, affective and processual. For Deleuze, 'to think is to experiment, and not, in the first place, to judge' (Rajchman 2001, 5). He puts experimentation before ontology; to connect is to experiment and explore the forces, intensities and flows prior to common-sense thinking. 'In other words', Rajchman writes, 'to make connections one needs not knowledge, certainty, or even ontology, but rather a trust that something may come out, though one is not yet completely sure what' (2001, 6–7).

Marguerite: Creative methods, art, performance and narrative can work well with this. Post-qualitative inquiry might work best to bring theory and method into a creative and experimental exchange that will help us think through our experiences.

Liezl: Yes, that could work, because our focus will be on the possibilities that emerge from theoretical and methodological tensions related to creating a research text.

Marguerite: While we do that, we need to situate this exploration within our specific context, where the call for decolonization in higher education has emerged strongly in recent years. Although this book is not about decolonization, it acknowledges the space from and in which our thinking emerges.

Liezl: Absolutely. In our context, the call for decolonization drives the call for rapid change and transformation in institutions of higher learning. Our understanding of decolonization is located in a specific, post-apartheid South Africa, however, we wish to extend it to larger global narratives of transformation and change within the higher education space.

Marguerite: In this sense, Achille Mbembe helps us to think about decolonization as a global issue. Mbembe (2016; 2019) draws a parallel between colonization, knowledge systems and mass data, which are all underpinned by principles of value extraction. Mbembe (2019) points to twenty-first century colonization as taking the shape of data extraction or data capturing, which commodifies our capacity for reasoning and critical thought. What does this mean for research on educator subjectivity? Research is so often data-driven. How do we resist a colonial tradition of sourcing, classifying and sorting information?

Liezl: Very important question. In a context of decolonization, we have to ask critical questions about the production of knowledge. How is it created, for whom, by whom and for what purpose? The theory and the method we use must help us ask and answer these questions.

Marguerite: Yes, our context demands that our engagement with knowledge is different. In a post-qualitative inquiry, we cannot think of knowledge as 'data' to be extracted for profit. We need to think of knowledge as that which is co-created for transformative purposes.

Book: I am shaped by their conversation. I am shaped by a context of rapid change. I am shaped by the calls for decolonization and transformation in higher education. I am shaped by the affects, flows and desires of those who came into existence long before my time, and I will continue to affect the lives of others, including yours, the reader who is reading me now. I am not alone. Since the #fallist movements in South Africa, there has been an explosion of published academic work that engages with the decolonization of South African higher education (Mbembe 2019), and what it might mean for curricula, pedagogy and practice (Jansen 2017a; 2017b; Le Grange 2018; Zembylas 2018). Many scholars have warned that the buzz around decolonization might lead to small changes in the content of what is taught (e.g. the incorporation of more African literature), but real change in pedagogy and epistemic assumptions may be limited (Keet 2014; Keet, Sattarzadeh and Munene 2017). The focus of this book is on educational research in the context of decolonization. Liezl and Marguerite situate their research on educator subjectivity within an understanding of method and theory as emerging, and it is not prescriptive. In research that allows the subversion of the power hierarchy, we need a theory and method that allow researchers to respond fluidly to the changing context.

Liezl: You know, sometimes I get the sense that I don't belong here.

Marguerite: What do you mean? *Where* don't you belong?

Liezl: I don't belong in the academic space. Other academics seem so well versed, so clear on what they think. I feel inadequate, almost stuck … in deep space.

Marguerite: Sometimes I also feel like an outsider, like I don't really connect to this space for so many reasons. I wonder if I am reading the 'right' articles, or if my work is really 'scholarly' enough. It is almost as if we are never 'good enough' in this space. Or at least, not the right kind of 'good' – if that makes any sense.

Liezl: Agreed. The higher education space can be very alienating. It makes me think of what the student movements of 2016 called for: not just financial access but epistemic access.

Marguerite: In other words, call for decolonization?

Liezl: I suppose so, but that is such a complex issue. What does it really mean? How do we think about educator subjectivity, and in relation to a call for a decolonized curriculum?

Marguerite: Let's consider the curriculum as lived (Aoki 2005; 1993), as located in experience (Eisner 1990), as a complicated conversation (Pinar 2012) and as autobiographical (Le Grange 2010). The educator and the curriculum becomes intertwined, and the boundaries between them fade away. Jansen (2017b, 169) states that 'teachers interpret the curriculum to students on the basis of their own experiences, backgrounds, politics and preferences'. Thus, the experiences of educators should play a pivotal role in working towards a decolonized curriculum. The manner in which we engage with those experiences is also significant in the context of decolonization.

Liezl: But what does it mean for us? You and I are quite literally the products of colonialism.

Marguerite: Yes, you and I are embedded in this context and in this research; we are the ones taking the snapshot, and where we stand will influence what we see. Who we are and how we fit into this story needs to be explored further. That will be done in Chapter 3.

Liezl: So, in order to situate ourselves, it will be necessary to explore our own autobiographical, non-linear processes of becoming educators?

Marguerite: Yes. And given the context we work in, we will need to engage with our whiteness through a critical lens. Even though we recognize that a racial lens is only one point of entry into a much larger assemblage of who we are, we also recognize that we cannot speak of decolonization without speaking of race. The one is embedded in the other. We cannot work or live in the context of change if we remain unchanged. The context demands us to be different.

Liezl: The personal and the professional are thus on a continuum, a fold where the subjectivity of the educator is constituted through the folding of the personal into the professional – the inside is a folded version of the outside. This notion of educator subjectivity is relevant to curriculum and pedagogy.

Marguerite: If we work within a critical pedagogical framework (Freire 2003), it becomes clear that educator identities and experiences are central to a transformative agenda. These experiences are framed within structural and systemic power relations that play out both inside and outside *classrooms and lecture halls.*

Liezl: We can, then, consider pedagogy as relational encounters that create opportunities for growth (Zembylas 2007), rather than classroom-bound practices. In thinking of a humanizing pedagogy, Zembylas (2018) refers to Freire (2003), who explained pedagogy as much more than teaching methods, and rather considered it as 'the entanglement of philosophy, politics and practice which demands that educators engage themselves and the students in transforming oppressive social conditions' (Zembylas 2018, 5). So, what this implies is that …

Marguerite: I'm sorry, but the noise outside is distracting me. Do you mind if we take a little break?

2.2 Noise

Liezl: Let's go and get a cup of coffee.

Book: As they exit the office, they see the door to a lecture hall at the end of the passage. A woman is sweeping a fine, dusty residue out the door. She is wearing a cleaner's uniform and a mask to protect her from the dust. The previous day, some students had emptied a fire extinguisher in the lecture hall. The incident relates to current protests by students who are waiting for their state funding to be paid out. The woman is sweeping and sweeping, but the yellow dust is spreading everywhere, making footprints all the way down the passageway as people walk past. They leave the building and walk past the construction site, towards the library, where a group of students is gathering at the entrance door. One student is using a megaphone to summon support for what seems to be a small-scale protest. Marguerite and Liezl walk past, hardly noticing. They are, by now, so used to the sounds of protesting students. Have they become desensitized? What do you lose and what do you gain in a process of transformation? Or is change just what it is and nothing more – a value-free and different mode of being than before? They were not always this nonchalant about student protests and social upheaval.

But in the current context of their work and lives, student protests have become part and parcel of the status quo. Much of this book will, in fact, centre on the wound, the moment of confrontation, such as the events at Shimla Park (Dick et al. 2019) and the affective incident on Liezl's *stoep* (porch) that will be narrated in Chapter 3. The ongoing event of protest will recur in Chapters 5, 6 and 7. In this context, the narratives of and sounds made by protesters are refrains of becomings, hauntings of the past and murmurs of possibly better futures.

Inside the coffee shop, pleasant smells wrap them in comfort and familiarity, which seem to keep the uneasiness at bay – at least for a while. Lebo smiles and waves from the other side of the room. She is sitting at a table with three other women: Nomsa, Deidre and Karabo. You will read more about these four women in Chapter 5, where we explain how they helped Liezl and Marguerite to think about educator subjectivity and the wound-event (see Section 5.2).

They sit down and order two cups of tea. Rooibos. Black. Bitter. Marguerite positions the laptop on the table between them. As they talk, they write. Book becomes both a participant and a consequence – both cause and effect – of their conversation.

> **Marguerite:** So, in our context, the autobiographical life, memory, history and daily life experiences of the educator become important areas of focus for research on social change and transformation.
> **Liezl:** Yes, but keeping in mind the call for decolonization … What does it mean for the educator? *How* or *what* or *who* should we be?

The sounds of soft coffee-shop jazz music is momentarily interrupted by a noise outside. Their hearts beat a little faster as the sound of the protesters outside gets louder. Somewhere, a siren sounds and intermingles with their uncomfortable memories of previous protest actions on campus. Marguerite fidgets with the napkin and folds it into some undefined shape as she tries to articulate her thoughts.

> **Marguerite:** If we look at the work of Mbembe (2016), he talks of the need to consider a plurality of knowledges when thinking of decolonization in education. Zembylas (2018) points to reconfiguring a humanizing pedagogy as decolonizing pedagogy by creating encounters that seek to challenge epistemic injustice and epistemic otherings (Keet 2014) in education settings.

Liezl: In other words, the call for change in education settings can be seen as a call for change in educators. A change in the way we do, think, practice and live. The aim of this book would, therefore, be to explore the entanglement of educator identity, pedagogy and practice in relation to change and transformation. But how do we explore this entanglement?

Marguerite: For me, the challenge is to find methodological approaches that are attuned to the complexity, entanglement, rationality and plurality of subjectivities in the context of transformation and change.

Liezl: You are talking about arts-based, narrative, collaborative and autobiographical methodologies?

Marguerite: Yes, although it would be pointless to fall back into a rigid understanding of what research methodology is or what it can do. We don't want to be captured by method (Manning 2015, 32). Instead, we want to embrace and explore different methodological tools to see what they might make possible as we respond to our experiences of being educators in a context of rapid change. In explaining a post-qualitative approach St. Pierre (2019, 4) asks, 'why do we think we should know what to do before we begin to inquire?' For St. Pierre, there is a distinct difference between inquiry and methodology. In writing about post-qualitative inquiry, she emphasizes that the goal is not to represent but rather to experiment and create new and novel ways of doing and knowing (2019, 4).

In Chapter 4, we will elaborate on this topic, as we explore arts-based inquiry as an affective research encounter. In Chapters 5 and 6, we look at how theory and methodology can help us explore becoming and educator subjectivity. In Chapter 5, we look at the story of four women and how their collective biography unfolds and connects rhizomatically. In Chapter 6, we use cartography to explore the process of becoming educators. Here, the narrative shifts to the transition from student to staff member that many young educators make.

The book interrupts their conversation. It turns their attention back to its pages and draws their eyes to its presence on the laptop screen:

Book: A Deleuzoguattarian notion of subjectivity as assembled and multiple requires an alternative methodological approach; traditional qualitative research methodologies used by the social sciences are designed to work with the notion of identity as given, centred, rational and fixed (Semetsky 2003, 221). In the words of Masny (2013, 241),

Regarding the subject, most research studies within modernity are based on the assumption of the autonomous thinking subject. The grounding of language, thought, and representation originates with a rational human being who is often referred to as the centered subject in a world that can be subjectively constructed. Deleuze moves away from the foundation of the subject who thinks and represents. Rather, it is the subject who is the product of events in life.

Book: Thus, subjectivity is no longer perceived as rational and centred but rather as affective and assembled, toppling the body/mind dualism. St. Pierre (2011) refers to post-qualitative research as the shift away from the Cartesian subject, towards a fluid, non-fixed assembled subject. In the assemblage, the subject is constituted through connections with other human and non-human entities, where none of these elements are more important than another. Novel connections in the assemblage are formed when elements are plugged into one another, where no pre-existing relations exist between these elements (Masny 2013, 330–41). They (Liezl and Marguerite) thus posit this research as post-qualitative, and this approach allows for a shift from the centred subject traditionally used in qualitative research towards an alternative understanding of subjectivity (Johansson 2016, 2). The post-qualitative shift also affects the ways in which research will be presented in this book. St. Pierre (2011, 613) criticizes qualitative research for being too normalizing and centralizing. Consequently, conventional and reductionist research is produced, which leaves little space for creating something radically new. Within qualitative research, certain methods and writing styles are perceived as conventional and acceptable. Honan and Bright (2016) aver that these methods of research and writing are exactly what Deleuze wants to move away from, as they are embedded in the traditional image of thought, which results in common-sense thinking habits. Although conventional qualitative research methods can, indeed, produce excellent research, it might, when followed and implemented too dogmatically, hinder creative thinking and novel research endeavours. Researchers might, hence, hesitate to write or think differently, which can result in the reproduction of the status quo. To contribute to improving society through conducting research, traditional thinking habits and writing styles should be challenged. To be able to really think is to be truly creative (Rajchman 2001, 5).

Marguerite: Would you like some more tea?

Liezl: No, I'm fine, thanks. We can, therefore, say that Deleuze and Guattari's notion of the subject and subjectivation makes it possible for us to embrace this post-qualitative approach to our research; in fact, it demands an alternative methodological approach. Throughout the book we seek to engage with subjectivity as an assembled and affective movement/performance, rather than a fixed entity. Furthermore, it is important to mention that Deleuze and Guattari's concepts should be viewed as processes, as something that should be performed. Their notions of assemblage and rhizome are particularly helpful for thinking in terms of connections and plugging in, rather than binary oppositions or linearity. These concepts are focused on movement and connection, rather than categorization, and therefore make it possible to contemplate becoming, rather than being (St. Pierre 2013, 226). Becoming, for example, is a rhizomatic process that contains horizontal tentacles that grow in unpredictable directions. In *A Thousand Plateaus*, Deleuze and Guattari write:

> [A]ny point of a rhizome can be connected to anything other, and must be. This is very different from the tree or root, which plots a point, fixes an order … An assemblage is precisely this increase in the dimensions of a multiplicity that necessarily changes in nature as it expands its connections. There are no points or positions in a rhizome, such as those found in a structure, tree, or root. There are only lines (2008, 7–8).

Marguerite: I see a clear link between post-qualitative inquiry and Deleuzoguattarian theory. It also seems to connect well with Mbembe's critique of knowledge systems as being 'underpinned by the logic of value extraction … Colonisation is going on when the world we inhabit is understood as a vast file of data awaiting extraction' (2019). So, throughout this book we will try to use theory and methodology that allow for subjectivity to emerge. We resist research practices that seem to extract 'data'. We do not want to represent or analyse, but rather to encounter. We do not want to replicate but rather open up to create difference.

Liezl: Deleuze and Guattari's thoughts and concepts allow for novel methods of knowledge production and make rendering new ways of understanding, doing and being in the world possible. Their theory enables us, as researchers, to experiment with empirical details, novel subjectivities and new connections between human and non-human entities (Mazzei 2014, 98; St. Pierre 2013, 226). In this way, we can produce knowledge that can respond to the context we find ourselves in.

Marguerite turns back to the screen. Her fingers stumble across the keyboard as she tries to capture what Liezl is saying. She types:

> Deleuze (2004a, 206) is critical of the traditional relationship between theory and methodology, where these two spheres are seen as incommensurable. This totalizing relationship inhibits theory and praxis from venturing from their prescriptive roles and, consequently, limits the evolution of what theory and praxis can be. Although Deleuze perceives theory as always local and related to a specific terrain or space, the rule of application of theory should not be limited to similar contexts. As soon as theory finds itself embedded or plugged into a terrain, it is confronted with obstacles, walls and clashes. This interaction with context, bodies, materiality and thought transforms the nature of theory and enables a migration to a different style of discourse and hence to a different domain. Deleuze describes the theory/praxis entanglement as an assemblage, where one theoretical point is relayed by another through praxis, while theory relays one practice to another. For theory to evolve, it has to hit a wall, while praxis has to break through this wall …

Marguerite: What you are saying is that theory makes it possible to think of the conflation of the educator's personal and professional experiences and how these entangle further with the space to create new ways of being. I also understand it to open up new possibilities for us to engage in a form of post-qualitative 'research creation' (Sweet, Nurminen, and Koro-Ljungberg 2019, 338).

Liezl: Yes, this entanglement of theory and methodology enables us, as researchers, to create and develop concepts and methodologies suitable for our specific context and research questions (Coleman and Ringrose 2014). Deleuze and Guattari's concepts will be viewed as tools that should be used to proliferate questions and becomings. Their concepts will be plugged into our material context, workshops, interviews, conversations and writing. What do the concepts make possible when they are plugged in? Does it make the creation of new concepts and novel subjectivities possible? These are questions that we aim to answer in our attempt to create new concepts for our material and immediate problems. In our research on subjectivity and social change at the UFS, we want to explore the research possibilities that Deleuze and Guattari's concepts open up. How can thinking with their concepts assist us to work towards novel ways of being and novel thoughts?

Marguerite: I am curious about arts-based and narrative methods and how they can inform a post-qualitative inquiry into educator subjectivity. In other words, how 'researchers can generate possibilities and becoming through the process of creating art in a purposefully relational manner' (Sweet et al. 2019, 338).

Liezl: We know in what direction we want to go, but where do we start?

Marguerite: Let's go for a walk.

They pay the bill and get up to leave.

Figure 4 Tea for two, 2019.
Photograph, Marguerite Müller.

Marguerite takes one of the little sugar packets and puts it in her handbag as they walk away.

Outside, the student protest that was staged earlier seems to have fizzled out. The crowd has dispersed and the library is open again. They walk across the campus, past the old buildings and the new buildings. In one window, they see a dead office plant looking out sadly at them. Liezl stubs her toe on the uneven surface of the pathway. They walk straight into Chapter 7. In this chapter, the subjectivity of place will be explored. Place is conceptualized as assembled, negotiated, always under construction and affective (Massey 2008), and consists of networks of human and non-human actors that continuously become-other as they come into relation to one another. It is envisioned that exploring these relations, and the terms of the construction of relations and the becomings they produce, will provide openings to consider personal/professional educator identity critically in terms of its materiality as it finds expression within a specific place. Chapter 7 will specifically consider the material, affective and spatial aspects of the recent calls for transformation, social change and decolonization by higher education institutions in South Africa.

2.3 What We Can Create

> **Marguerite:** Look at this exhibition: Roots, rhizomes and radicles, an exhibition by Cecilia Maartens.
> **Liezl:** You still have some time before you need to get back to the office? Let's go to this exhibition.

When they enter the exhibition space, they are drawn to a large botanical rhizomatic installation in the middle of the gallery. The artist, Cecilia Maartens, has suspended the organic rhizomatic matter in the air so that it fills up the gallery. We read the artist's statement:

> In reaction to a complaint from my neighbour that the giant reeds in my backyard are invading his property, I decided to dig up the roots along the fence. In the process I discovered the roots are the most amazing rhizomes that grew in multiple directions turning and twirling their way between, over and under other roots, forming an intricate network. The theoretic comprehension of the peculiar growth modalities of the rhizome was practically demonstrated! I enthusiastically excavated more and more rhizomes. I decided to use these miraculously formed objects to produce an artwork to depict a metaphorical

Figure 5 Liezl and the rhizome, 2019.
Photograph: Marguerite Müller. Artwork courtesy: Cecilia Maartens, a presentiment, 2018, Installation of dried roots from the giant reed plant, 240 × 220 × 180 cm.

glimpse into the inner life of interconnecting, forming of new pathways (sometimes with difficulty). The growing process of the rhizome is furthermore analogous to human life interwoven with multi-dimensional environments, shaping our lives as we continuously form relationships and new perspectives, apprehending the future in terms of the experiences of the past. Bergson (1908: 197)[1] explains this process using a cone (memories pile up in the past, which comprise the body of the cone) and are actualized in the present through intuition (i.e. at the point of the cone). The installation has deliberately been assembled in the shape of Bergson's drawing of a memory cone and represents one's life being implanted in time and memories intertwined with nature and one's environment. The deeper pain and disappointments of life are explored in the installation through the burrs of the withering plant. (Maartens-Van Vuuren 2019)[2]

For us, the rhizome became a visual metaphor of how we connect theory and methodology in this book. The artwork by Cecilia Maartens helped us to think of our research as a type of 'excavation' of rhizomatic matter. The connections and formations are already there, but we need to look for it, find it, dig it out. At the same time, we used these formations to create something, an installation, a story, a construction, a book. Our aim with this dual process of excavation and creation is to show how the theory of Deleuze and Guattari entangles with postqualitative, narrative, arts-based inquiry, so that we could think in a processual manner about professional educator subjectivity in relation to rapid social change.

As we left the art exhibition, each of us went our own way. Marguerite went back to her office. Taking the packet of sugar out of her handbag, she read the words printed on the back.

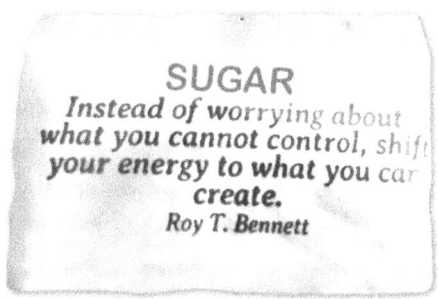

Figure 6 What you cannot control, 2019.
Photograph, Marguerite Müller.

Book: So, this is how they start writing. They are creating me: Book. They are writing together. Their collaboration stretches over years. Often, they meet for tea, or just sit in Marguerite's office, staring out the window. Sometimes, they walk and talk. Subjectivity is shaped by, amongst other things, time, context and encounter. They exchange emails and WhatsApp messages, they take snapshots, collect little scraps of paper with writing on it and, eventually, learn how to use video chat. They attend conferences together. They eat dinner together. They experience a national lockdown and are stuck in different parts of the country, far apart. Often they agree, and often they don't. Writing together is not a smooth or linear process. Sometimes they are on the same page, sometimes not. Writing a book does not take place in a vacuum; it takes place in the messy, complex, mundane, extraordinary real world of everyday life. As they are writing me, their lives go on: work, teaching, marking, meetings, kids, love, anxiety, job applications, laundry, rejections, travels, a pandemic… In the epilogue (Chapter 9), this background noise, which often informed the process of writing together over many years, unfolds. The epilogue is a reflective piece, in which Marguerite and Liezl show how the process of writing together unfolded and how it opened up possibilities for being and thinking differently, together.

2.4 Writing a Book … Together

How do you write a book together?

We do not intend to give you the answer to that question, because it will be different for every writing collaboration. However, we will share some of the 'backgrounds' of our writing process in the epilogue. The point is that we went into this collaboration because writing a book was a 'first' for both of us and it seemed a little less scary to do it together.

Also, here are some of the things we learned from our co-authoring journey:

1. *Keep a journal.* Keep a journal of your entire process, from the beginning to the end. Writing does not happen outside of life. Write down *everything*, even if it seems trivial at the time. Where you are, what you smell, what you hear, what you see, how you feel – *everything*. WhatsApp messages, emails, silly screenshots of video chat meetings. In the end, this will become the glue that binds your journey.
2. *Meet regularly.* Even if it is virtually. The more you meet, the more your ideas will grow.
3. *Be brave.* Don't be scared. Be experimental. In the end, you will have to delete most of what you have written. That is OK, since the good stuff always seems to resurface.
4. *Save everything in a cloud. Never* think I will save this later. Save it *now*.
5. *Trust each other.* There is nothing more important than trust. Know that when I get tired, you will pick up and vice versa. Two is better than one – we can share the burden.
6. *Laugh and cry as much as you can, or need to* – about life, at each other, at how difficult it is to write a book. Laugh about the WhatsApp pictures and messages of four years ago, when you really didn't have a clue. You are putting a substantial part of your days on this earth into this text, into this book. Make sure you enjoy the journey. Make sure it is worth it.
7. *Remember that your words are unlikely to change the world, but you will certainly change yourself in this process.* And maybe that is enough.

3

A Tale of the Assembled Subject: Exploring Whiteness

3.1 Shut Up and Listen

Let's be honest. You might have to probably ask yourself the following question: What do these two white chicks have to say about decolonization anyway? Aren't they the cause of the problem?

Despite the derogatory gender marker, it is a valid question that has, in the course of writing this book, been put to us. We have also been asked similar questions in different forms and in various settings.

Though this book is not about race, writing about subjectivity cannot happen outside identity markers, including race. We are people with histories. Most of that history is highly problematic and not very nice, but we need to own up to it anyway.

In the space where we work, we are often confronted with our whiteness. Once, at a conference, we were asked, 'why do *you* think you can come into *this* space and talk about race?'

Often, during engagements with students we have been reminded, white people should really just shut up and listen.

We agree. We understand how our context corresponds to movements such as #BlackLivesMatter. White people, like us, should really shut up. And listen.

We do not support #AllLivesMatter. We do not support colour-blind ideologies that mask centuries of racist ideology and colonial exploitation. Neither do we advertise our assumed wokeness on social media. We find that irritating and often pretentious. Perhaps it is necessary, and some people must do it, but that is not our job. Our job is to write. We write, and listen, and think, and write, and write, and talk about what we have written and then start all over again. We hope that all this writing helps to heal some of all the brokenness and hurt and anger and pain that exist in the world.

We know that working in a setting so tainted by the residue of colonial and apartheid legacies really makes us, as white South Africans, complicit in years and years of structural racial oppression. Our complicity is not a personal choice but a historical consequence – it is something we need to accept and live with. It is also something we need to work actively against, something we need to seek to change. Sometimes, keeping quiet and listening is the best way to do that. We cannot risk getting defensive about our own complicity in the unequal situation that persists along races in our country and worldwide. We caused this situation. Not us, personally, but those who share our marker: our whiteness.

In this chapter, we will write about our experiences, because, in the end, we think there is also a complicity, or even privilege in silence. Keeping quiet is, indeed, so much easier than talking about the past, and the present, and our own problematic selves. Talking is painful and it exposes us and makes us vulnerable. Silence can disguise who we are and what we think; it can keep us safe. Writing about yourself is risky. We have encountered that risk. Once you put something on paper, it is there in black on white. You have nowhere to hide once the words hit the page, or even worse, if those words are published.

In this chapter, we will present ourselves as more than one-dimensional. We do not defend who we are. We are composite creatures, entangled in a complex connection to the space we find ourselves in. We belong and we don't belong. In fact, we don't really know if belonging is an option anymore. There is just being and becoming.

3.2 Assembling Our Parts

In the following section, we will present a collaborative, performative narrative that is located in memories of our experiences as residence managers at the UFS, Bloemfontein, South Africa. We use memory as an entry point into the micro-social experiences of educator subjectivities in the context of transformation. We reflect on our experiences as support staff members living on campus during a time of student protests. Our reflection also comes from our PhD work, which dealt with educator and student identity during a time of rapid transformation. Through our work and studies, we were placed in the unique position of experiencing how the traditional personal/professional educator identity binary was disrupted and conflated. By critically reflecting on our subjectivities/identities and looking into whiteness, we position ourselves in a larger narrative of transformation. Reading ourselves as assembled subjects, we find expression in the non-linear narrative of affective becomings. In the following performative text, we use visual images and dialogue to disrupt the Cartesian subject through a collaborative writing process. We created the performative text through a process of collaborative autobiographical writing. We drew pictures of our experiences and lives that lead up to a certain critical incident. Then, we used our drawings to create a collaborative narrative of our experiences. The research assemblage we will present here is a non-linear conversation that developed through our drawings, writings, conversations and presentations on this work. The conversation is between the two of us, but we also invite a voice of critique (Critic), and a theoretical voice (as narrated by Book), to engage in and disrupt our dialogue, which results in a performance of multiplicity.

3.3 Setting the Stage

Book: 'The two of us wrote Anti-Oedipus together. Since each of us was several, there was already quite a crowd. Here we have made use of everything that came within range, what was closest as well as farthest away. We have assigned clever pseudonyms to prevent recognition'. (Deleuze and Guattari 2008, 3)

Marguerite: We chose to be two characters in a story. The story of Daisy and Pinkovski. Our story is a story that starts during a time of turmoil at the UFS. We use pseudonyms to access the different aspects of ourselves that evolved during that time. Our memories are used to explore our current expressions of being through the construction of past events.
Liezl: By using this performative style of writing, we also highlight the non-linearity and multiplicity of our subjectivities and its becoming.
Critic: Just don't get upset if I ask you some uncomfortable questions – that is *my* job.
Marguerite: So, where does our story begin?

3.3.1 Scene 1: I'm Sorry

Pinkovski: It begins on the *stoep* of the Madelief residence, located next to the university's main gate, where I worked and lived for six years. #RhodesMustFall, #FeesMustFall and student protests had flamed up. The first #FeesMustFall protest showed potential to really unite black and white students, although white students did not participate, which highlighted the persistent material and cultural differences between the students. Then, #Shimlapark happened. One of the Madelief students told me that white rugby spectators went onto the field to beat up black protesters who had disrupted the game. The girls came running back to the residence, worried that the black students would damage their cars in retaliation. It was open season on white men. Most of the white girls moved out of the residence. At one stage, I was confronted by a group of protesters on the *stoep* of the residence. They were looking for the white boyfriend of one of the girls, as he was hiding in the residence; the boyfriend had come onto campus to fetch a friend when protesters targeted his car, slashed the tyres and chased him into the residence. The girls called me and said there was trouble on the *stoep*. I went out and saw the Student Representative Council talking to the protesters. Lerato, a previous prime (leader) of the residence, came to me and said we should keep the boy inside, as the protesters want to hurt him. Somebody asked, 'Who's got a key?' A finger pointed to me.

Figure 7 I'm sorry, 2018.
Pencil drawing, Liezl Dick.

The next moment, I was surrounded by a crowd of protesters. 'We demand you bring that guy out, or we'll trash this residence! I was hit last night by 50 whites!' 'I am sorry about that', I said. 'Whatever!', was the group's response. So much intensity and anger. I started to shiver. In that moment, I realized how my white skin limited the way I was perceived.

Critic: I do find it interesting that you were surprised by the actions of the protesters. You do have the same face as the oppressor, after all, and you have to remember that. Steve Biko (in Stubbs 1987, 71–2) said, 'No matter how genuine a liberal's motivations may be, he has to accept that, although he did not choose to be born into privilege, the blacks cannot but be suspicious of his motives'. In turn, Fanon avers that 'I am overdetermined from without. I am the slave not of the "idea" that others have of me but of my own appearance' (Fanon 2007, 95). Why is it, then, that the limitations of your white skin were only realized on your *stoep*? This could be described as a classic example of white privilege and, most of all, white ignorance and racial illiteracy (Burke 2011).

Pinkovski: Shimla Park was devastating for everyone. It felt like the racial integration had collapsed and was nullified. The line between black and white was drawn. I experienced total disillusionment. The protesting students were arrested in front of my residence. I had to hide the students, who were also protesters, from the police. Private security was deployed. The campus was fenced off with barbed wire. It felt like a war zone. The residence managers were the foot soldiers, dealing with the violence while receiving very little instruction from line managers or support from top management. We did not know when the unrest would end; it felt like it could continue for a very long time. I suppose it was always unavoidable that something like this would happen. Goodbye, rainbow nation?

3.3.2 Scene 2: Do You Think This Is Real?

Daisy: My story began one summer evening in 2016. We were having a residence meeting with some of the student leaders and, suddenly, they all checked something on their phones. They showed me the #Shimlapark video of white spectators attacking black protesters on the rugby field earlier that evening. It looked unreal and I even asked one student, 'Do you think this is real?' That night, the UFS Bloemfontein campus turned into chaos and it became very real, and I became very scared. The students clashed with police in front of the residence. The next morning, I left campus with my family. I was worried about their safety. I was also eight months pregnant and worried about access to campus. Later, when I came back, I realized that the students were also scared. The white students were scared of the black protesters, and the black students were scared of radical white Afrikaner groups. A lot of things were being shared on social media – a lot of threats. It was a time of fear and racial polarization. After that, it felt like we were in a circle of traumatic events and violence for the rest of that year. By the time of the #FeesMustFall protest of October 2016, my baby had been born and I was walking with her outside when police vehicles chased after students and arrested them right in front of me.

Figure 8 Do you think this is real? 2018.
Pencil drawing and photograph, Marguerite Müller.

I felt unable to protect the students and worried about the safety of my baby. That evening, I saw students provoke the police by throwing bottles; the police reacted by firing rubber bullets. It happened right outside my children's bedroom window, and I was glad he did not wake up. The next morning, we picked up rubber bullet casings outside the front door. When I took my son to school, he wanted to know why there were riot police at the gate. I became very anxious and questioned everything. At the time I also became frustrated with university management, because it felt like they gave instructions and made decisions which we had to communicate to large groups of angry students, even though we had little authority. We were stuck in the middle, between the students and management, in a very volatile situation. Nothing of my academic background in education or my professional experience in education contexts had prepared me to handle this volatile situation.

Critic: You are telling the story of a violent and traumatic event. You position yourselves as white women who work in contexts where your racial identities influence your personal and professional experiences. Given the racial history of South Africa and your positionality, you are part of the history of white supremacy. Should you even be doing this type of research?

Daisy: What do you mean?

Critic: In your narrative, it seems as if the pain of black bodies only becomes visible or relevant when seen through white eyes. Are you aware of your blind spots, as white people, and do those blind spots make it impossible for you to do socially just research on transformation? In the narrative, the moment of trauma for you is when you witness the direct violence to the black body. A violence that had, prior to this event, been erased through the conscious act of 'not seeing'. This is a neglected dimension of whiteness – the different acts of seeing and not seeing violence.

Pinkovski: I sense a lot of pain, Critic. So, do you think we did not see before? Are we looking for redemption? Are we confronting the possibility that the perpetrators look like us?

Book: I think what Critic means is that you need to acknowledge the ignorance contract that played such an integral role in upholding white supremacy. Steyn (2012, 8) describes the ignorance contract as

> the tacit agreement to entertain ignorance [that] lies at the heart of a society structured in racial hierarchy. Unlike the conventional theorization of ignorance that regards ignorance as a matter of faulty individual cognition, or a collective absence of yet-to-be-acquired knowledge, ignorance is understood as a social achievement with strategic value. The apartheid narratives illustrate that for ignorance to function as social

regulation, subjectivities must be formed that are appropriate performers of ignorance, disciplined in cognition, affect and ethics. Both white and black South Africans produced epistemologies of ignorance, although the terms of the contract were set by white society as the group with the dominant power.

Daisy: We understand the need to acknowledge our positionality as white South Africans. But does it limit what we can write and research?
Pinkovski: How do we deal with our whiteness and our past in an accountable way, without essentializing ourselves and others?
Critic: How did you become essentialized?

3.3.3 Scene 3: The Personal/Professional Binary Unravels

Daisy: I was born in the 1980s, in apartheid South Africa. I went to a 'good' Afrikaans school and received a 'good' education. On Sundays, my family went to the Dutch Reformed Church where my father was a *Dominee* (minister) and after the service, I attended Sunday school. I was part of a close-knit community where similar views on religion, politics, history, and a shared language served as the glue that bound us together as white Afrikaners. The only people of colour we knew were those who worked as cleaners or gardeners. I suppose I lived a protected life.
Pinkovski: Your story is also mine. Church and religion were very important. Sunday was the day my father worked, and we went to church twice. Our house was next to the church and my childhood was carefree. The only black people I knew were Katie, our nanny, and Jacob Pyle and Sidwell October, who participated in marathons with my father.
Daisy: Our childhood experiences were probably similar to those of many other white South Africans growing up in the 1980s.
Critic: Aren't your early childhood memories more complicated than this? Weren't you aware of the performativity of whiteness?
Pinkovski: I remember, we went to the sea once and Katie was not allowed to swim with us. It's also interesting that we didn't call the marathon guys *Oom* (Uncle) Jacob and *Oom* Sidwell, as we would have called white adults. Although I was a child, I was vaguely aware that some people were different from me even then and that they were also perceived as less of a person by my society.

Figure 9 Growing up in the 1980s, 2018.
Pencil drawing and watercolour, Liezl Dick and Marguerite Müller.

Critic: Is this how whiteness informed your formative years?
Daisy: I remember, when I was in the sixth grade, the principal called all of us to the hall and announced that the first student of colour would be coming to our school the next day and that we must all behave well. Looking back it seems so strange and absurd that we were being prepped for the arrival of an 11-year-old girl.

When I went to high school in 1996, South Africa was two years into a new democracy. The country had a new flag, a new president, a new constitution and a new South African Schools Act that would combat 'racism and sexism and all other forms of unfair discrimination and intolerance' (Republic of South Africa 1996, 1). For the first time, I sat in school classrooms shoulder-to-shoulder with coloured[1] Afrikaans speakers. My coloured classmates did not live in white neighbourhoods but in the township that had been designated for coloured people under

Figure 10 Straight lines, 2014.
Pen drawing, Marguerite Müller.

>   the apartheid legislation and which was quite some distance from
>   school. They arrived in buses in the morning and left in the afternoon.
>   In class, we became friends and exchanged ideas on topics from music
>   to religion. But when the bell rang for break, the coloured learners sat in
>   one group, and I would sit with other white learners. The teachers were
>   all white and the cleaners were all black. The principal was male and the
>   secretaries were all female.
> **Critic:** Your white guilt is useless to me. Are you avoiding my question? Is
>   this how white supremacy and the patriarchy gets transmitted?
> **Pinkovski:** 1994 was exciting – a feeling of possibility was in the air.
>   New flag, new languages, a rainbow nation. After completing school,
>   I enrolled at university and studied philosophy. In retrospect, it is
>   interesting that we never discussed race or read the works of black
>   philosophers. Most lecturers were white and Afrikaans, except
>   for one coloured woman. I drank a lot of Black Label (beer) and

started questioning everything, from religion to social expectations. Stellenbosch was still a very white space and even in the lecture rooms we were mostly white students, and most classes were in Afrikaans. I became very angry and I was not entirely sure why. Then I left for the Netherlands on an airplane, where white supremacy was also rife.

Figure 11 And then I left, 2018.
Pencil drawing, Liezl Dick.

Daisy: I think we construct our memories to show how our identities were shaped in a context of structural oppression and racialization.

Pinkovski: But our story is not just one of ignorance, it is also one of becoming. How can we become less essentialized and move away from white supremacy if we essentialize ourselves or are essentialized by society? How do we become other?

Book: Are you arguing that whiteness is caught up in binary identity politics? Erasmus (2017, 95–7) avers that the only way to 'disturb the scaffolding of hegemonic meanings attached to blackness and whiteness' is to find 'new meanings and performances of whiteness and blackness' and to allow it to emerge. New ways of understanding whiteness are possible but can only manifest if new ways of being white are lived and performed (Erasmus 2017).

Daisy: So, by becoming the assembled subject, we can acknowledge whiteness as a construct in which we might become essentialized but also move beyond it as we become a multiplicity. We disturb racial categories without taking a colour-blind approach, or denying the material impact of these categories. We do not deny our whiteness, but we do explore becomings beyond whiteness.

Book: You are entering the assembled, nomadic subject as multiplicity. You might find the idea of the nomad very helpful. Nomad subjectivity makes it possible to travel from one identity to another, from one way of looking at the world to another, moving away from the Cartesian, centred subject, towards an understanding of subjectivity that allows for several identities to be inhabited at the same time. The nomad is not limited by borders, but transgresses differences (Braidotti 2011b). The nomad travels from one narrative to another, allowing different narratives/identities/subjectivities to co-exist without contradictions. The implication of the nomad subjectivity on the personal/professional educator identity is that this identity becomes a continuum and the parts are connected, not separate from each another. The nomad helps us to think in terms of identity beyond binary opposites. In other words, you are not either just an educator or just a person with a private life and personal history. You are both at the same time, and this understanding has an impact on your practice as an educator.

Daisy: So, we are using a memory web similar to an assemblage, which helps us to work with our memories in a non-linear way. Memory and experience become a way to explore micro-social experiences as affective becomings of multiplicities of educator identity through a narrative inquiry.

Pinkovski: Can this understanding of subjectivity help us to disrupt the professional/personal binary?

Daisy: I think this is where the narrative becomes useful, the collaborative act of writing our memories helps us to see connections that would not be possible otherwise. By working with a professional/personal educator identity continuum – rather than the professional and the personal as oppositions – we can investigate the way this continuum helps us to work towards transformation.

Book: 'Whenever we love justice and stand on the side of justice, we refuse simplistic binaries. We refuse to allow either/or thinking to cloud our judgement. We embrace the logic of both/and. We acknowledge the limits of what we know' (hooks 2003, 10).

Pinkovski: So, the question is not what our memories mean, but what they make possible. If we want to use memory as a way to make non-linear connections between the personal and the professional, we need to work collaboratively. It is only through collaboration and radical relationality that we can move beyond the simplistic binary of self and other.

Daisy: What is radical relationality?

Book: Braidotti (2011a, 313) defines radical relationality as 'an ethical life [that] pursues that which enhances and strengthens the subject without reference to transcendental values but rather in the awareness of one's interconnection with others'.

Pinkovski: So, back on my *stoep*, I could feel the anger of the protesters penetrating my body. The anger caused by violence against the black body was projected onto me, with my white body. Is this what is happening? And what happened next highlighted the value of what Rosi Braidotti (2011a) calls 'radical relationality' in my narrative: I heard someone in the crowd saying, 'Don't hurt this lady', and the next moment I hear someone else say, 'Hello, Pinkovski. Why do you look so worried?' It's my friend Tshepo, who was part of the protester group, coming to me and giving me a hug. This gesture disturbed the confrontation between me and the protesters. Tshepo's hug disturbed the binary opposites of race that had been created in the micro-social space on the *stoep*. For a moment, the situation is defused.

Daisy: Now I understand what you mean. I remember being scared for myself and my family after the Shimla Park incident. I was worried because we are white and the students in the residence where I work are mostly black. After the night of police and student clashes on campus, I left the campus with my family. Later that day I received a text from one of the residence students, saying, 'Don't worry, we will protect you and your family'. The student was saying she would protect me even though it was actually my job to protect her. In that moment I realized I had to return, to be there for the students. Our white and black binaries no longer seemed to define our roles.

Pinkovski: We should not underestimate the importance of radical relationality. Proper connections and relationships might be our only hope in becoming more than our racialized subjectivities. Our moments of trauma are prominent in our narrative – the memory that compels us to write.

Daisy: And when we think of those memories, it opens up a new web of memories that extends to our childhoods, but also stretches out to our professional experiences in education. What other connections happen in this memory web?

Pinkovski: I remember, when I initially started working at the residence, I realized how little I knew about South Africa and its people.

Daisy: I think I experienced that when I went to travel and work after university. And then, returning to South Africa was just as challenging, because, suddenly, it was like seeing my own country for the first time. I felt like home was a foreign space. I needed to understand my own social identity better in order to teach learners who are very different from me. I decided to do a PhD in order to explore the deep, dark, impenetrable forest of the unknown within me.

Pinkovski: I was frustrated and didn't know how to fulfil the complex role of being a residence manager in a multicultural space. I decided that, to cope, I had to focus more on the PhD, which I decided to do on the racial integration of the residence. Living in such close proximity with girls representing various cultures and races made me painfully aware of the problematics of race and racialization in South Africa. In order to do my job as residence manager, I had to question my own personal identity as a white Afrikaner. It was no longer possible to keep the personal and the professional apart – the one informed the other.

3.4 What's the Use of Writing about Ourselves?

Our aim with the performative text is to explore how our personal and professional identities informed each other in our roles as residence heads and researchers. By analysing whiteness as one aspect of the assembled subject, we perform the way identity oscillates between being essentialized and assembled. Our life stories became our work stories. The narrative approach to our identities, as assembled and multiple, helped us think of subjectivity as multiple 'storyscape'. In this way, it becomes possible to make new connections and become aware of the entanglement of our becomings. This chapter takes the form of an assemblage where theory and methodology, and our narratives, are plugged into one another, making new connections and becomings possible, while also creating new narratives. In this performative text, our narratives are not singular. Our experiences are not linear. Sometimes, we make sense of our complex identities, and sometimes we feel frustrated, reduced and essentialized. Through the memory web, which also functions as an assemblage, we explored how our experiences of being white South African women have informed and shaped our identities during a time of rapid social change.

In writing about ourselves, we show how a collaborative, performative narrative might highlight subjectivity as affective becoming. In this way, we hope to create a way to disrupt and conflate the personal/professional educator identity. By reflecting critically on our subjectivities/identities and by looking into whiteness, we position ourselves in a larger narrative of transformation. By reading ourselves as assembled subjects, we trouble the professional/personal educator binary, in order to create new possibilities of responding to a changing higher education context. We rely on a research assemblage, where theory and methodology become entangled, in line with an ontology that gives preference to multiplicity, difference and becoming. The question we work with is, how can we use theory and methodology to think differently about our own subjectivity during a time of rapid change? We do not attempt to answer this question but rather use it as a catalyst to demonstrate how our lives were shaped by the context we grew up in, and the context we work in now. The flows and affects shaped our subjectivities and continue to do so. We understand subjectivity as a process, and we respond to the process through creation.

3.5 Creating a Performative Text

We found it useful to create a collaborative autobiographical narrative to engage with our experiences and connect the experiences to theory. We used drawings, dialogue and performative writing to explore how our personal life histories came to impact our professional lives. Since we were working with the idea of a research assemblage, we included multiple voices in one performative text (Dick et al. 2019). We 'cast' ourselves as two characters in a performance and then we 'cast' the voice of Book as theory and the voice of Critic as a response to the narrative. Here, we outline our process for creating a performative narrative as a research text. We also offer some questions to challenge the reader to contemplate what the research assemblage makes possible through reflection on their own experiences.

1. Draw Your Storyboard

Question: Can you describe/draw six critical incidents that shaped or influenced who you are today?

Draw a storyboard of about six frames/scenes to highlight some critical incidents in your personal/professional history.

2. Share Verbally with Each Other

Question: How have the critical incidents in your life shaped your becoming?

Share your drawing or storyboard with a partner. Explain verbally what you drew and why. In turn, listen to their narrative.

3. Write a Collaborative Text

Question: How can our different experiences connect, meet and entangle to form one narrative?

Write a collaborative text in which your separate narratives 'meet' to become part of one story.

4. Read the Text Defractively

Question: How can collaborative narrative biography/memory work help us to reflect critically and engage with a theory to formulate a research text?

Read the performative text you created to see how it connects to the relevant research texts. Then read the different texts through each other – defractively (Barad 2003) – to see how they connect.

5. Rewrite to Engage with Theoretical Perspectives

Question: How can we respond to the theoretical perspectives in this text?
Create a 'voice' for theory in your performative text.

6. Perform the Text for an Audience

Questions: How does the audience change our text? How does the audience respond to us? How do we respond to the audience? What triggers you? What triggers the audience?

Perform the text for an audience. Find an audience that will be critical of what you are doing and saying – academic conference audiences could work. A group of colleagues, family members or neighbours could also work. Record verbal critical feedback. Also seek written critical feedback, if possible. The more critical feedback you get, the better. Even if it hurts.

7. Rewrite after Listening to Your Audience

Question: What are the blind spots in your narrative? What do you choose to ignore? What makes you uncomfortable? Why do you try to present yourself in a certain way? What triggers you?
Create a 'voice' for criticism in your performative text. Let the criticism you receive become part of the work. Engage with it instead of running away from it (even if you want to).

8. Reflect

Reflect on the entire process and how it connects to your research question.
Our guiding question: How can the creation of a performative text of the assembled subject help us think creatively and beyond binaries towards becoming during a time of social change?

9. Repeat Steps 1–8

4

Finding What You Have Not Yet Lost: An Affective Inquiry into Educator Subjectivity

If you don't know it's impossible it's easier to do. And because nobody's done it before they haven't made up rules to stop anyone doing that again yet

– Gaiman (2018)

Marguerite: Liezl once gave me a gift; a notebook with blank pages. A book with blank pages is the absolute best gift to receive because it has so many possibilities. However, when I opened it, I felt a little intimidated by the blank pages in front of me. What did these pages want from me? I put the notebook aside and I reached for another book Liezl had left on my desk, a borrowed 'gift'. This one contained many words. Words about *Deleuze and Research Methodologies* (Coleman and Ringrose 2014). What did these words want from me, I wondered? It was just as intimidating as the empty pages. Were these words even meant for *me*? I spent a lot of time reading and rereading without really grasping much of what the words said. It took me some time to remember that, for me, understanding comes simultaneously with doing. Theory emerges with method and does not precede it.

4.1 Writing a Book

When we began writing this book, it was because we thought we had something to say, not because we knew how to say it. In fact, neither of us had written a book before and no one had written *this* book before. The Chinese philosopher Confucius is credited for the proverbial words, 'I hear and I forget, I see and

I remember, I do and I understand' (Vaillancourt 2009, 272). Therefore, in this chapter, we wanted to focus on doing, and how it sometimes leads to understanding and sometimes to creation. As we started writing, and talking, and drawing, and walking, the book showed itself. We met Book as much as we wrote a book. It crept out of the margins of our attempts to pin it down. Book became a character in our lives – present and absent, fictional and real and always already simultaneously present in the future and in the past. We learned that Book could not be forced into existence but deserved time and space to show itself. Doing happens in time; it is constrained by time but also shaped by it: linear time, non-linear time, deep time, meaningful time, empty time, timeless time. We had to harness every kind of time to get this done, in time, and on time. Book became an event. So, meeting Book was a lot like making art or doodling on a blank page (which is also art) in response to all the words we read, conversations we had and walks we took. It was an affective encounter that branched out into many directions and helped us make new connections. In this chapter, we will explain how we met Book through a process of using arts-based inquiry into educator subjectivity during a time of social change. In this chapter, we will start by explaining what we understand arts-based inquiry to be. Then, we will show how we used it. Finally, we will reflect on how our method of inquiry was informed by theory.

4.2 Using Arts-Based Inquiry

To enquire is to enter into dialogue with the world. Gert Biesta, in his book, *Letting Art Teach*, argues that 'the educational question of "how to come and remain in dialogue with the world – is also the question of art"' (2017, 38). He uses the work of Hannah Arendt who (re)defined understanding as an 'unending activity by which, in constant change and variation, we come to terms with and reconcile ourselves to reality, that is, try to be at home in world' (1994, 307–8). Thus, when we enquire, we try to be at home in the world through dialogue encounters with the world. In this encounter, 'the world does not simply appear as an object of our manipulations and interpretations, but can exist in its own integrity and in dialogue with us' (Biesta 2017, 37). A dialogue is not a one-way interaction. When we dialogue, we participate and give as much as we receive. For this reason, inquiry cannot just be about understanding, finding or interpretation but is also about receiving and learning and changing. Biesta (2017, 39) helps us to think of art, education and inquiry as closely related. He shifts the understanding of art, from art being a passive object to interpret (how can I make sense of this?) to art as agentic (what is this asking of me?). In doing so, he emphasizes that art (and education and inquiry) is not centred around us and our understanding but is rather something that moves us to be different and act differently.

The work of Biesta provides a theoretical lens for looking at art as an agentic force that can move us into conversation with the world. Thus, 'painting, sculpture, dance and music are not just different ways of "doing" art, not just different forms of art, but first and foremost different ways of being in dialogue with the world that have the potential to teach us a range of different lessons of what it means to exist as subject in and with the world' (Biesta 2017, 112).

In our inquiry, we are concerned with educator subjectivity during a time of social change. Using an arts-based inquiry is useful because it allows us to think of subjectivity as multiple, assembled and fluid. Arts-based inquiry also helps us to frame our inquiry as a dialogue with the world. The purpose of inquiry then is not to solve problems and find answers but rather to help us linger in the encounter with the world because 'the arts try to show us this predicament of our existence – that not everything makes sense, that not everything can be resolved – and urge us to stay with the predicament rather than to run away from it' (Biesta 2017, 98).

The predicament (Biesta 2017), uncertainty, tension and discomfort (Eisner 2008) in our context was precisely what drew us to arts-based research inquiry. We started writing this book during the #FeesMustFall student movement that swept through higher education in 2016 and led to campuses across the country being shut down for extended periods. We finished this book during the COVID-19 pandemic of 2020. The national South African lockdown was implemented at the onset of the COVID-19 pandemic in March 2020 and had the strange effect of bringing us back to our first encounter with this book. In a way, it reawakened our connection to where it all started: shutdown. Amidst a national lockdown, or campus shutdown, there is a moment in time when life derails from the illusion of 'normal' to a place where we stand as outsiders looking in. This sudden change, like a campus shutdown or national lockdown, can sometimes amplify the normal-everyday-taken-for-granted things that we usually overlook. Sometimes, it is precisely the absence of things that can sometimes make them more present.

Throughout the process of writing and researching this book, we have been attuned to the particular details of our situation. We have thus been looking for the normal-everyday-taken-for-granted in our own lives and the lives of those who participated in the study. This approach to education research has its roots in narrative inquiry (Chase 2011; Clandinin and Connelly 2000), which we view as narrowly entwined with arts-based inquiry.

If we trace the history of arts-based research in education, it takes us to the work of Elliot Eisner on education criticism, Tom Barone on narrative storytelling and Sara Lawrence Lightfoot on portraiture (Cahnmann-Taylor and Siegesmund 2017, 6). Arts-based research made it possible to explore the blurred lines between art and science in research inquiry. The goal of arts-based inquiry is, first, to gain new insights and new questions rather than absolute answers, second, to recognize the blurred lines between self and other and, lastly, to speak to diverse audiences within and outside the academy (Cahnmann-Taylor and Siegesmund 2017, 9).

In narrative inquiry, the personal stories of the everyday lives of teachers and students become entry points into the social context and education field. Similarly, in arts-based inquiry, the general resides in the particular (Eisner 2008, 20). We thus purposefully explored affective incidents and encounters of personal narrative in order to respond to a complex and challenging moment in the South African higher education landscape.

McNiff illuminates a clear connection between creation (of art) and the process of inquiry:

> Perhaps a defining quality of art-based researchers is their willingness to start the work with questions and a willingness to design methods in response to the particular situation, as contrasted to the more general contemporary tendency within the human sciences to fit the question into a fixed research method. The art of the art-based researcher extends to the creation of a process of inquiry. (2008, 33)

In our inquiry, we wanted to create meaning from our experiences (instead of looking for meaning in experience) because we did not want to get stuck in repetitive ways of dealing with difficulties. Therefore, we did not engage in a research inquiry that seeks to understand but rather in one that aimed to create different ways of knowing and allowed us to enter into dialogue with the world. This form of inquiry helped us to respond to the everyday and mundane experiences in our lives as well as the unexpected predicaments and critical incidents we encountered. Also, knowing through art helped us to give up a measure of control over the research process and to be open to surprise and the unexpected (McNiff 2008, 40).

We situated our inquiry within a post-qualitative (St. Pierre 2019) approach because we did not wish to fit our inquiry into any pre-existing research framework but rather allow the process itself to shape the outcome. It is important to be aware of the process of creation that forms part of the research assemblage. The process and method do not stand separately from the site or the participants in a study. In a post-qualitative inquiry, its focus on more complex ways of knowing and being result in alternative epistemologies that respond to the complexity of educator identity and subjectivity in the context of social change and transformation in education. Within this transformative paradigm, the aim is to produce knowledge that transforms society and addresses social inequality. The research is thus action-oriented and demands that we produce something new – not just a new way of understanding but also knowledge that makes a new way of doing possible. The educator is seen as a significant role player in the social context and, therefore, the study focused on educator experiences and educator subjectivity. This focus is in line with a narrative tradition in education research that focuses on educator identity and experience as key elements in shaping education contexts and change.

As we outline the research design, we wish to paint a frame for the way we will structure our inquiry and at the same time acknowledge that the process of inquiry will be one that allows for methodological inventiveness to emerge in our responses to new questions that might arise on our research journey. Change requires us to respond in novel and inventive ways. Our research methods should echo our unique and novel responses (Müller 2020, 44). Finley (2012, 72) explains that arts-based research values affective and embodied experience and encourages the researcher to 'create meaning from experience', attend to the form of knowledge that is created and function in in-between spaces. For this reason, arts-based research troubles the traditional science/art divide and challenges 'institutionalized classist, racist, and colonializing ways of experiencing and discoursing about human experience' (Finley 2012, 73). Through arts-based inquiry, our research can and should be taken outside of traditional enclaves of academic knowledge to new audiences as 'socially responsible research for and by the people cannot reside inside the lonely walls of academic institutions' (Finley 2012, 74). Furthermore, 'arts-based educational research can contribute significantly to a re-visioning of education' (Eisner 2008, 26). The re-visioning is made possible by focusing on imagination of what might be made possible through research inquiry. Finley states that 'critical arts-based research makes intentional use of imagination. It is a performative research methodology that is structured on the notion of possibility, what might be, of a research tradition that is postcolonial, pluralistic, ethical, and transformative in positive ways' (2017, 561).

Working with an arts-based inquiry means that the research design needs a measure of flexibility and space for growth and change. It was important for us that the methods we used responded to the context and the participants in a way that allowed us to change and rethink our design as the project developed. While allowing space for fluidity and change in our methods of data collection and interpretation, we paid close attention to the aesthetics at every step and phase of our work. Eisner warns against neglecting aesthetics in arts-based research by saying that 'the distinguishing feature of arts-based research is that it uses aesthetic qualities to shed light on the educational situations we care about. Arts-based research is not simply the application of a variety of loose methods; it is the result of artistically crafting the description of the situation so that it can be seen from another angle' (2008, 22).

We, therefore, approached the writing of this book as we would approach the crafting of an artwork. This artwork/book had to emerge within an intricate tension that exists, in our context, between the sticky residue of colonization and the calls for decolonization. We wanted to understand and see educator subjectivity from another angle and we needed a theory and method that would allow us to do so. Arts-based inquiry allowed us to plug into the concepts of the event, assemblage, multiplicity, cartography and affect to see HOW these can help us engage with – and think differently and authentically about – educator subjectivity during a time of social change. Furthermore, it allowed us to respond to our contextual situation by giving us a way to pursue feminist, decolonial and pluralistic forms of knowledges. In this way we hoped to 'reject research practices that are implicated in paternalistic and colonizing traditions, or that treat production and acquisition of knowledge as a function of social privilege' (Finley 2012, 75). Instead, our aim was to embark on research encounters that create 'reflective dialogue and meaningful action and, thereby, to change the world in positive ways that contribute to progressive, participatory, and ethical social action' (Finley 2012, 75). Arts-based inquiry helped us to enter into an affective dialogue with the world. In the following section, we will explain how we used arts-based inquiry and how it helped us evolve our research question.

4.3 This Is What We Did

Book did not fall from thin air. Book was the result of a series of research encounters that stretched over approximately five years. We approached our research process in a rhizomatic rather than linear way. Our arts-based inquiry made it possible to move between research encounters as we were guided by affect. Some of the research encounters were planned and others emerged. We allowed our process to grow and change organically as we also grew and changed as researchers. Much of the material we used to write this book emerged from our doctoral research projects (Dick 2016; Müller 2016). However, our doctoral work only formed a base from which we could enter into conversation with each other during a time of shared experiences in our work environment and challenging context. Our process of inquiry was fuelled by friendship, which meant that the business of writing a book also became the business of life, sharing life on this planet and in our specific context. We began our journey by sharing our own becomings. Thereafter, we organized three workshops of two hours each, which served as research encounters with educators at the UFS. The workshops were followed by four smaller focus group discussions with participants who attended the workshops. While the workshops offered us a broader perspective of educator subjectivity in our context, the focus groups allowed us to video chat into more specific critical incidents and affective becoming. Throughout, we made use of arts-based methods of inquiry and the narratives that emerged informed our creation of Chapters 5 and 6.

4.3.1 Planning

The first workshop was developed for staff and students who work in the Division of Student Affairs at the UFS. In this workshop, we aimed to use affective incidents as a point of entry into educators' understanding of the self and their entanglement with students, colleagues and the university context. Through an exploration of collective experiential knowledge, we posit affect as an integral part of professional knowledge. By doing this, we hope to open up the possibility for multiple aspects of identity to emerge and conflate as we engage with social identity categories, such as race, gender, class and so on. Through the use of affect, we hope to demonstrate the possibilities of a personal/professional educator identity continuum in education for social change.

The second and third workshops were designed in a similar way to the first one. However, after each workshop, we made some changes to the design and question, as our understanding and learning shifted. The workshops were intended to obtain a sense of the experiences of a group of educators at the UFS. The term educator in our work is not restricted to academic or teaching staff but also encompasses support staff and student leadership who are people entering into pedagogical relationships with students. Before we embarked on the process of data generation, we obtained ethics clearance to conduct research with staff and students at the UFS. All participants were informed of our research project before the workshops and signed informed consent to participate.

In addition to the workshops, we held four focus group discussions. We invited four to six participants to a focus group discussion of two hours, and each presented over lunchtime. The participants we invited were all educators at the UFS. We invited certain participants in workshop 1 to participate in further focus group discussions. These participants were invited due to the roles they had played in the workshop as well as because of their involvement in campus life at the time of the 2016 protests. For each group, we invited a different set of participants. For groups 2 and 3, we invited educators who had recently moved from being students to being staff members. Most of the participants in groups 1, 2 and 3 had been student leaders during the 2016 protests and had moved on from being students to being employees of the UFS by the time we facilitated the discussions. We believed that this group of participants could give unique insights into the blurred lines between educator and student subjectivity. The experiences of this group are written into the arts-based narratives of Chapter 6. For focus group 4, we invited some more experienced staff members who had been around for some years. The group of participants who accepted our invitation turned out to be a group of women; their narrative is reported in Chapter 5. Our final research encounter, as discussed in Chapter 7, was with the space and place itself. We used cartography and walking to guide our dialogue with the non-human and more-than-human research elements that constituted the setting, physical space and memory of our research site.

4.3.2 Doing

We designed and presented a workshop on professional development to be presented during a Student Affairs colloquium (Müller and Dick 2019) at the UFS: *Creative Arts-Based Workshop on Educator Identity, Development and Transformative Pedagogy.* The workshop was attended by forty participants who work for different student support structures at the UFS as well as some academic lecturers and students. Before the workshop, all the participants signed informed consent forms to allow us to make use of the audio recordings of discussions and conversations during the workshop, as well as the images of the artworks they created. We introduced our research project to the participants by explaining that we were working on a book project called *Subjectivity and Social Change in Higher Education: A Collaborative Arts-Based Narrative*. Next, we gave the participants a short introduction to the idea of transformed pedagogy as a humanistic (Jama 2017) or humanizing (Zembylas 2018) pedagogy, which can be described as a form of critical pedagogy (Freire 2003). A humanizing approach to pedagogy means that 'educators, therefore, are responsible for creating the conditions suitable to promoting a more fully human world through their pedagogical practices' (Zembylas 2018, 5). The introduction helped us to frame our stance, namely that educators are embedded in processes of change and transformation. We went on to discuss the process of arts-based inquiry into educators experiences and how 'the arts are particularly powerful to promote the creative and transformational processes that are essential for professional identity development, including reflection and reflexivity on self' (McKay and Sappa 2019). Thereafter, we asked educators to reflect on critical incidents that they have experienced at the UFS. We asked them to write a short reflection piece or make a reflection drawing, in which they address the question: *How do you see yourself as an educator in relation to a specific challenge or experience you have encountered in this context?*

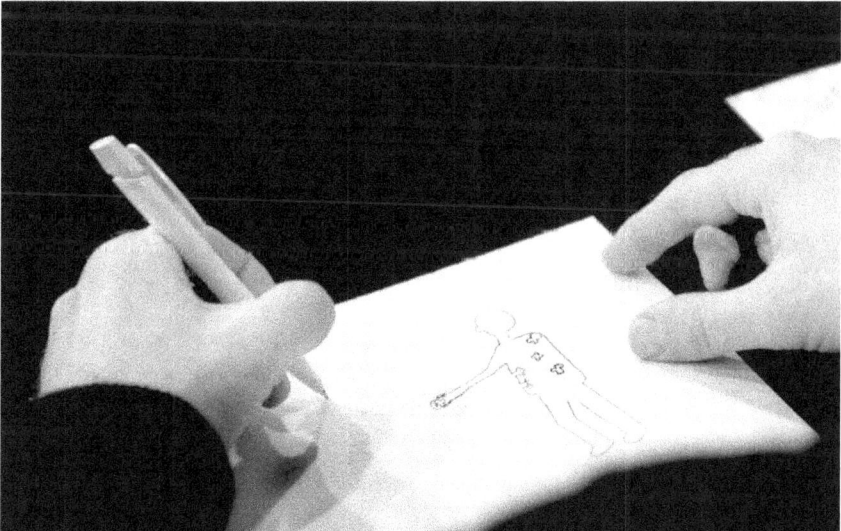

Figure 12 What do I make possible? 2019.
Photograph, Marguerite Müller.

Then, we asked the individual participants to form groups of four to six members, in which they were encouraged to share their individual reflections. They were then invited to create a collaborative artwork, as a group, in which they expressed their responses to the following question: *What change do we (as educators) make possible and how are we changed in this context?* Each group was given a bag filled with a variety of construction and art materials, which included coloured paper, toilet rolls, empty cardboard boxes, coloured stickers, glue, scissors, markers, sticky tape, masking tape, toothpicks, sponges, rope and wool.

We emphasized that there were no rules, and we tried to put participants at ease with the arts-based approach by emphasizing that it was not about the artworks' appearance but rather about what they communicated. We recorded their conversations throughout the creative process and, at the end, everyone participated in a gallery walk where different groups had the opportunity to exhibit and explain their final artwork. We ended the workshop with a reflection writing exercise, in which participants could share their insights and experiences of the workshop and what it might tell us about educator subjectivity during a time of social change. Finally, we had a group reflection session on what the workshop had made possible.

4.3.3 Finding a Poem

After the workshop, we got together to collaboratively interpret the 'data' that had been generated during the workshop. We use the word data very cautiously, as we acknowledge that, with a post-qualitative design, words such as data and analysis become problematic because of the implicit assumptions of representational logic on which they rely (Müller 2020, 44). Post-qualitative inquiry is strongly influenced by post-structural theories that resist the ontological assumption of a real world out there that can, in any way, be represented in research (Denzin 2013). St. Pierre (2013) advocates for a post-qualitative inquiry in which the focus shifts from data gathering and analysis to more affective connections with research encounters. The possibilities for what can serve as data, and how it can be interpreted, are thus also expanded. As Marguerite found in her PhD work,

> This kind of creative and affective collaborative interpretation is a move away from what traditionally counts as empirical data and analysis to interrogate the traditional power hierarchies that exist in research. A move towards decolonised ways of doing research is also a move towards research practices that do not rely on binaries, hierarchies, categories, and labels to make sense of experiences. (Müller 2016, 99)

We would, therefore, like to offer our sense-making of the experiences that were shared during research encounters as we engaged with workshop 1. As we worked through the written reflections participants had shared with us, we came across the 'gift', an artwork, a beautiful poem that a participant had written, and it opened up a sensory and embodied connection to our inquiry.

> May I be open for what you have not yet lost
> I see
> I hear
> I feel
> I am
> Are you too?
>
> But I know you are
> Because I am
> I know I am
> Because we are
> May we find each other
> Through each other
>
> May we transcend our animal
> And collectively enlight
> During peace and during fright
>
> I wish to share my suffering and to connect to yours
> For I know we are both human
> Yet we often do not see each other
> In the shadow of our ivory tower
> May I impart something useful, for I have been walking and experiencing for a little longer
> And may I be open for what you have not yet lost,
> that I may hold onto it as I continue onto the path.

The poem helped us to think of educator subjectivity as embodied, entangled, affective, critical, hopeful and resilient. In response to the poem, we created our own creative response using the written reflections on how educators saw themselves in relation to a specific challenge or experience they had encountered in the UFS context. After we read the reflections, we listened to the recordings and wrote down the parts of the conversation that stood out as significant in terms of our research question: *What change do we (as educators) make possible and how are we changed in this context?* In the following section, we will render these conversations in a visual and poetic form of research reporting (Pithouse-Morgan, Madondo and Grossi 2019).

4.3.4 Listening to Voices

We used a number of written responses and reworked them into dialogue format. The voices in this dialogue are fictional (Eliastam et al. 2019), although they were drawn from real responses that had emerged in the workshop. The conversation is a composite of different voices that had emerged during the workshop. We walked through their words and we met four characters: a lecturer, a professor, a student assistant and a researcher. We also make use of a choir of voices that responds to the conversation. Finally, we include some images of the artworks created during the workshop.

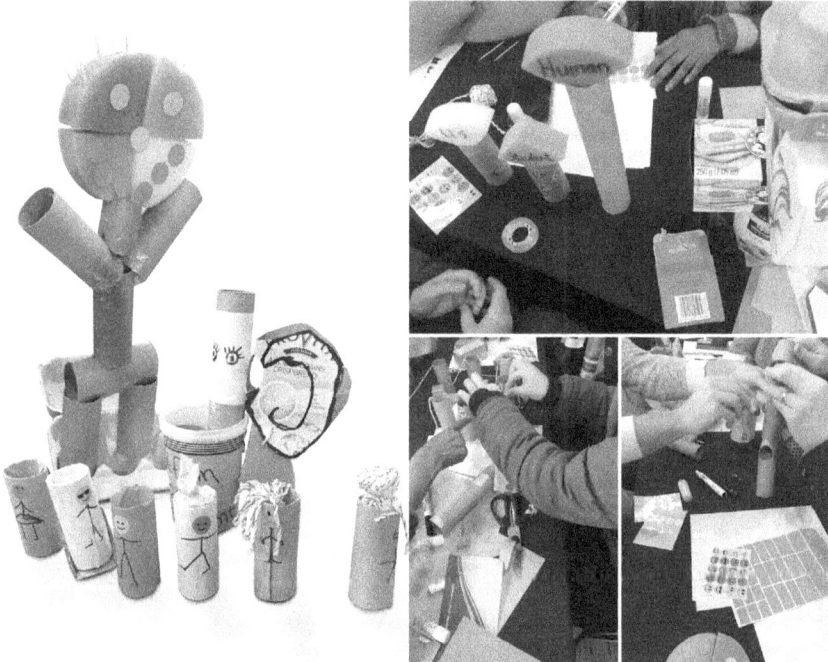

Figure 13 Who we are and what we do, 2019.
Multimedia installations co-created by workshop participants.

> **Researcher:** How do you see yourself as an educator in relation to a specific challenge or experience you have encountered in this context?
> **Professor**: The educator and student are co-creators of knowledge.
> **Researcher:** And each have diverse experiences, diverse backgrounds, and come from diverse communities.
> **Student assistant:** Where educators have to break the hierarchy of power to allow co-creation of knowledge.

Lecturer: Where students may face challenges and fall behind, but the community, the circle, has the power to lift those who fall.

Choir of voices:
We need a big ear
to listen and learn
as we break the power hierarchy
and create a full human experience
in a reciprocal process of learning
the context want us to listen more
but we are only able to hear a select few,
and some of the messages come, but it is unclear …

Professor: As an educator, I need to stand my ground. Students have limitations, but also endless potential, and we need to unlock the potential. I need to unlock the world for my students.
Student assistant: Embrace the child within. In the circle of learning we share, learn, unlearn, relearn.
Lecturer: An ant on its feet can do more than an elephant lying down.
Researcher: I am not huge, but I can make a big impact. Knowing myself, understanding myself, guiding, with wisdom, clearly, with direction.
Professor: We need to claim the space as the professional educator during the time of transformation.
Lecturer: There are many forces competing for the students' attention, and there are many ways they can go astray. I have to recognize the problems and intervene at the places where the students can falter.
Assistant: I believe myself to be a bridge between students and their overall well-being. It is important to listen to the student voice on the ground, in that way we will be able to hear their cries and provide and guide towards the right solutions.

Choir of voices:
We need to build a platform of opportunity
Students come from diverse backgrounds and we need to find where they are standing before moving them somewhere else
When I come to varsity I was …. sad, uncertain, unsure,
We come from a place of unknowing,
It felt like I was lacking
But at university you grow and start find out who you are as a person
We need to help them realize – this is who I am

So that going out into real world
They are now confident

Professor: Decisions have consequences, and we need to prepare students to know how to handle consequences, because they lack coping resources and resilience.
Researcher: They have difficulty dealing with everyday life?
Lecturer: The current students demand immediate gratification. They have a great sense of entitlement. They lack facing responsibility for their own actions or decisions.
Student assistant: We are instilling hope. We need to meet as co-workers to engage each other about how the environment is changing us so that we can strengthen our collaborative efforts.
Professor: I see myself at the centre.
Lecturer: But you need to hear their voice, listen without judging.
Student assistant: Bring light in the dark, bring hope.
Researcher: I bring light during difficult discussions. Our role is to build others.
Professor: I feel burdened to give guidance, information and advice to students who look at issues in a way far different from my view.
Lecturer: Giving of self toward the wholeness and development of others, ultimately enlarges the self

Because we bring the experience.

Choir of voices:
Think of the academy as a tall tower
When students come here they wonder, how do you reach that?
Students experiencing challenges during their time with us
And it affect us as humans in terms of supporting each other
learning growth, learning, experience, compassion, warmth.

Student assistant: Listen, listen, listen. We bring hope and change. We bring hope and change by listening to students' needs. We facilitate discussions and dialogues about issues of concern and find a solution together.
Researcher: As educators, we also need to be in conversation with one another to learn from each other to assist our students better. So the student can be a flower that flourishes.

Professor: I see myself as a point of stability when environments fluctuate. I am a clear example of values that stay the same in a changing environment.

Lecturer: I see myself a someone who transfers my lived experiences as knowledge to students in their life situations.

Student assistant: Change is happening and we have to adapt to it. Adapt to changes to assist the students.

Professor: We are responsible for students and their reaction to change. Creating a safe space of students to learn.

Lecturer: Only a person who has a strong heart and patience for students can survive.

Researcher: Where are we now with transformation?

Student assistant: Transformation is not a means to end but a way of life.

Choir of voices:
We need to be the light
We must be the solution that the students are asking for
We are in a space that flourishes on human interaction
We create opportunity for engagement …
We are mediators
Our main objective is to dispel the notion that there is nothing that can be done
We instil hope, regardless of what is going on inside of you, whether you feel hopeless or not,
You need to put on that brave face for the students, it is a self-fulfilling prophecy
By showing hope they will eventually realize there is hope.

A participant wrote a letter to Liezl and Marguerite after the arts-based workshop:

Hi Liezl & Marguerite,

I wanted to share this with you.

Reflecting on the overall process, the individual/small group activities I enjoyed the most. Not having a dominant personality makes it more difficult to share my opinions, compared to smaller groups. A factor that I felt affected this group activity negatively is the fact that office dynamics rolls over into these type of activities. Sharing freely without judgement/rejection/negative comments from my line manager was difficult. Therefore, I would like to give my input on reflecting on the whole process of hope and resiliency.

I believe hope can be created when I help someone explore any possible alternatives to giving up. Creating a caring and approachable space for students to open up and share their difficulties could help the student to create their own hope for the future. Resiliency is a skill I believe that can be developed. People can learn resiliency by what they observe, and if they grew up in families who stayed strong regardless of difficult challenges, they see that it can be done. Unfortunately the university system 'give in' too easily with demands from students via protests etc., which enables students. This leads to students rather complaining as means of getting out the easy way, than to endure uncomfortability and persevering. This spoon-feeding culture cycle needs to be broken, and universities across the country would need to make that difficult decision to stop giving students what they want, but rather focus on what they need and what might be a fair compromise. However, that is a lot easier said than done! It is such a complex issue. Regardless of the environment an individual grew up in, resiliency remains each individual's responsibility. The view they take of difficulties might be an easy first step to work towards resiliency. Instead of having a victim mentality such as 'Why me?', people can rather move to growth and ask 'What can I learn from this?'

4.3.5 What Did We Learn?

From the collaborative artworks we learned that educators in our context constructed themselves as being, among others, people who can listen (the big ear), people who can create opportunities (the platform), people who can guide the students (this is who I am), people who lead by example (a little bit taller), and people who instil hope (the light). We were also interested in how the participants experienced the workshop and what it made possible for them. Therefore, at the end of the workshop, we asked the participants what they had learned. Participants wrote about what they had learned in the process of creation. Our question was, what did they take away from the workshop if/how they thought of their educator role differently? Below are some of the reflections participants shared:

> So often we focus on what we give or the contribution we make … we forget it is also a self-fulfilling prophecy … we also grow and develop and develop our own professional competencies – otherwise we become despondent and drained … and we … as we give of ourselves
>
> One realizes that you need to engage a little bit more … I realize that we all feel that the context in higher education wants us not to tell all the time, but to listen.
>
> Thanks for using the arts as a medium … it is daunting – you think it has to be a certain why – we forget the symbolism of what we build. We should all see ourselves as educators and you can use different methods to influence what you

want to do – we fall in a trap of doing things in one way … using one method to achieve something, but this is something one can do if you want to go deeper if you want to get meaning from your students, surveys and questionnaires might not help you to get what you need so this methodology can help you to get deep data.

From these responses, we conclude that the participants mostly reacted positively to our arts-based methods. However, we experienced both successes and challenges during the first workshop. We used these to rethink and redesign our subsequent workshops and focus groups. First of all, we realized that, when planning an arts-based workshop, it is important to consider the inclusivity of all the activities. For example, in workshop 1, we had a blind participant who could not read the consent form and had trouble participating in the construction activity. In following workshops and focus groups, we ensured that we made the consent forms available per email ahead of time so that participants could report issues and we also ensured that the arts-based activities we planned would not exclude any person due to disability.

Regarding the actual construction activity, we noticed that many of the artworks depicted the 'educator' as a big figure that towers over smaller students. The educator was often represented almost like a supernatural or superhuman force that should guide and help the student – be the light. Despite our question about specific experiences, most of the participants focused on very general descriptions of the educator and almost no one referred to specific incidents. The participants seemed focused on discussing and representing their roles as educators and very few engaged with the question, how are you changed? Many participants commented on the importance of listening and how that is central to the role of the educator; in fact, one group even created a giant ear as their artwork to emphasize this point. The role and actions of the educator seemed to dominate the discussion in such a way that we walked away with the impression that the student is almost seen as a passive recipient of assistance and help. In the workshop, which was attended by both staff and students, the idea of the educator as agentic/active and the student as a passive recipient of help came across quite clearly. Despite this, the metaphor of knowledge exchange between the student and the educator also emerged. Several groups mentioned the circle of knowledge and how the educator and the student share knowledge. Another theme that emerged was the holistic development of the student, but this was often mentioned within a particular discourse of holistic development where the student was seen as lacking, and after attending university, where the student was seen as lacking when they enter the university and as whole when they leave.

During the workshop, we observed that people were engaged and involved in the construction process and seemed to have fun working in their groups. At the end of the workshop, many participants commented on how the creative process was enjoyable and useful. Although the creative arts-based approach was well received, we realized that the creative process itself did not necessarily lead to critical engagement with self. One of the issues we identified was that participants seemed keen to represent themselves as 'ideal' selves. This urge prevented the educators from engaging with the difficulty and complexity of social change and personal transformation. The educators represented themselves as almost superhuman, whole and complete, whereas the students were depicted as precisely the opposite. After the workshop, we reflected that there was almost a reluctance or fear to admit how daunting the space we work in is. The question we had hoped to answer was, what change do we (as educators) make possible and how are we changed in this context? Yet, at the end of the workshop, we found little engagement with that specific question and we had to re-evaluate our question as well as our methods. The question evolved into, What does change in the context teach us as educators?

The fact that we had a big group of educators and students who function in a power hierarchy within the institution undoubtedly had an effect on the presentation of the educators as almost 'superhuman', lacking vulnerability and always in control. We found this to be in contrast to the emerging narratives in our context, namely that we needed to move away from hierarchies of power and towards the decolonization of our university space. We became aware of a very fixed, rigid view of how and what educators are perceived to be, and what their role is, for example, providing light and preventing students from venturing on the wrong path. We also noticed that participants refrained from using very specific examples of personal change, or of how they were changed by affective incidents, or what change they make possible as educators. Their feedback was vague, and it sounded as if they regurgitated phrases that one would find in institutional policy documents, which did not reflect the dynamic change happening in everyday life on campus. We wanted to know how to get a more relational and less static reading and understanding of educator subjectivity. However, some of the poems and drawings gave us more affective material to work with, for example, the poem at the beginning of this section, *May I be open for what you have not yet lost*. This poem helped us to think of the educator as embodied, entangled, affective, critical, hopeful and resilient. In addition, the collaborative artworks helped us to think of the educator as someone who can listen, create opportunities, guide, instil hope and lead by example. We found that overall the use of arts-based inquiry helped us engage in affective research encounters that could create new and authentic ways of thinking about professional educator subjectivity in relation to rapid social change.

We used this to guide our design of subsequent workshops and focus groups. We tailored our designs so that we could video chat in more closely to the lived micro-moments and move away from grand narratives of what educators might think they *should* be or what they think is *expected*. In follow-up focus groups we also made an effort to invite many participants who had moved from a student role to an educator role in recent years. This group was particularly relevant to our study, because they were able to use lived experiences to give a more nuanced and complex reading (from the student and educator side) and were able to critically engage with questions about institutional change and what it meant to be an educator during a time of social change.

We thus found that arts-based methods of research helped us to engage with the affective dimensions of educator subjectivity. However, at the same time, we realized that the design must be fine-tuned and revised in order to work well. Although the methods were well received and participants responded positively to the research encounter, we found that the use of arts-based methods did not necessarily guarantee the kind of reflective engagement we had hoped for. The question we set out to answer is, how do you see yourself as an educator in relation to a specific challenge or experience you have encountered in this context? However, through the process of inquiry, the question evolved to become, what does social change ask from us in the context of education?

We found that affective arts-based inquiry is not a research method for solving problems and finding solutions. Arts-based research is, however, helpful for understanding the complexity of educator subjectivity and the education context. We set out to get a glimpse into the space between experience and understanding, between theory and method, and between problems and solutions. In this way, arts-based inquiry helped us in our research on educator subjectivity during a time of social change. In the following chapters, we will explore in more depth how this method spoke to our theoretical understanding of subjectivity and also what arts-based inquiry made possible in our study.

4.4 An Affective Encounter

I sit down and open the notebook with blank pages. In front of me is a stack of articles and books that will help me fill these pages. Where should I start? The answer comes from Biesta (2017, 39): 'Our relationship with the world is not a matter of intention, but rather of affection.'

During the above-mentioned workshop we tried to think of educator subjectivity as an affective assemblage: a *mixed masala*[1] of difference, in which affect refers to the changes in what human and more-than-human 'bodies' are capable of. 'It is a degree of power held within any given assemblage, or 'mixture'. Affects extend or decrease the limits of what a 'body' – or a given assemblage or mixture – can do' (Hickey-Moody 2014, 80). So, how can affect inform our inquiry into educator subjectivity?

As embodied subjectivities we encounter the world, and in each encounter or interaction, there is a gain or loss (Hickey-Moody 2014, 79) of affect as a result of the encounter or interaction. Therefore, our research inquiry was attuned to the affective encounters that constantly shaped and reshaped the assemblage. During the workshop, the participants engaged with each other and with different materials, cutting and pasting things together to create artworks. These creative groupwork engagements were affective incidents, where ideas and emotions were shared, bodies connected with one another and with all sorts of materials that were used to create and build. What did these engagements make possible? And what can the artworks tell us about educator subjectivity and experiences?

Let's think of the assemblage as an artwork. Biesta (2017) tells us that we should not try to understand the artwork as much as we should allow it to 'teach us'. Similarly, Hickey-Moody explains affective pedagogy as the 'concept that aesthetics teach us by changing how we feel [and how] this awareness can be brought into research' (2014, 79). Our research inquiry is thus not a one-way street – a process of asking questions and finding answers. In fact, we are not trying to understand educator subjectivity and pin it down with representative logic. We do not view it as a phenomenon we can represent, analyse and understand. Instead, we are searching for a way to become attuned to the affective encounters with educators and how these encounters cause different subjectivities to emerge.

My young daughter crawls onto my lap. She snuggles up against me and I breathe in the sweet smell of her hair as I continue reading over her shoulder: 'Thus affect is the materiality of change: it is "the passage from one state to another" which occurs in relation to "affecting bodies"' (Hickey-Moody 2014, 81). I reach for my phone to message Liezl with one hand: So I am an assemblage, an assembled subjectivity, each encounter I have with the world is an affective incident that creates the possibility for change?

Liezl is typing. While I wait for her response, I show my daughter a video on Facebook: A montage of animals roaming free all over the world during a time we are all locked inside due to COVID-19. Animals roaming around the places once dominated by humans. *Liezl is* still *typing*, so I read on.

Figure 14 Liezl is typing, 2020.
Screenshot of Marguerite's phone.

> Human bodies are constantly re-making themselves through their actions: relations, interests, the context in which they live ... this remaking can be understood as the form of art that bodies produce and consume, as these are technologies of subjectivation and ways of learning about the world. Aesthetic sensibilities are a means through which we become who we are and they are how we learn. (Hickey-Moody 2014, 82)

Don't try to make sense of this, I think. Just meet it, encounter it; allow it to affect you. I doodle in my notebook for a while with my daughter. When we view affect as embedded and intertwined with our method of doing research and in our research encounters, then our process of making, crafting and responding can be seen as both practical and political. Our 'aesthetic responsiveness' (Hickey-Moody 2014, 85) thus becomes a way of mapping out the *possible* in our social imaginings. Our 'aesthetic sensibilities' that are crafted through our artful engagement with the research process make change possible – in research but also in the social imagination.

I look out of the window to the now-empty lawns that stretch across this institution of higher education. I think of the presence of absence: the absence of students from campus during the lockdown. Absence can fill so much space in our lives. The most obvious example is the absence of a loved one. Suddenly

I think of the letter I never received. It was around 2008 when I was living in South Korea, and my grandmother had sent me a handwritten letter all the way from South Africa. She was already in her nineties by then, and it was the last letter she ever sent me. But I never received it. It did actually reach the school where I worked, but the colleague who received the mail mistakenly threw it away, not able to decipher my grandmother's writing on the envelope and failing to realize it was intended for me. The absence of my grandmother's last handwritten letter to me is something I still carry around with me. I linger in that empty space as I look out the window. The thing that never happened. Like my 10-year-old son who was all packed for a school camp the night before the national COVID-19 lockdown was announced. Now he talks about it constantly – the camp to which he never went. Its absence fills his thoughts, fires his imagination of *what if*. What if I had received that letter, what if he did go to the camp and what if there were students on campus now? How would the world be different? And what should we do with these *what if's*? 'Through crafting physical fragments of imagined worlds, artworks make new realities possible, the impacts and effects of which research in the humanities and social sciences is particularly well disposed to map' (Hickey-Moody 2014, 85).

My daughter is playing with a Band-Aid on her knee. She is learning how to ride her bike and had fallen that morning. There had been some crying, but the Elsa (character in *Frozen II*) plaster helped a lot. Art is presence that reminds us of absence, and affect lies somewhere in between. Like a wound; both permanent and temporary. Both hurting and healing.

I read on. My eyes are drawn to a sentence that Liezl had underlined in pencil: 'Art is a mode of producing subjectivity' (Hickey-Moody 2014, 88). A little further down the page she had underlined another sentence with a squiggly line: 'A work of art is pedagogical to the extent it crafts new elements of difference and is able to imbue them on its spectator' (Hickey-Moody 2014, 88). I wonder why she used a squiggly line instead of a straight line.

We learn through the encounter with art, but we also learn through the creation of art. 'The production of art requires opening up to chaos, a line of deterritorialisation that cracks open what they call a territorial refrain and connects to other spaces (rhizome), other melodies. This connection, facilitated by opening up to chaos, forms a chorus' (Hickey-Moody 2014, 89).

When art ruptures the surface of the text, it draws our attention away from the textual world, to the assemblage of which it forms part. Perhaps this is what I would like to draw attention to in my engagement with Hickey-Moody's work (2014) on affect and affective pedagogy. My reading of her work was devoid of space and time. It was, in fact, filled with human and more-than-human encounters that interrupted and redirected my attention and thinking. In this chapter, I attempted to sketch my affective encounter with the text as an artwork, rather than something I need to understand. 'Subjective change is part of a broader assemblage of social change that is activated by the production of new aesthetic milieus. Research needs to better understand and illustrate how *affectus*, the rhythmic trace of the world incorporated into a body-becoming, makes new geographies of meaning' (Hickey-Moody 2014, 93).

Thinking about this, my gaze falls again on the empty lawn outside my window. It is sunny and green, and inviting. Soon, I will walk outside, to meet it, to feel it beneath my feet.

In our inquiry into educator subjectivity, it is important to remember that 'focusing on the affective assemblages of research contexts: the smells, sounds aesthetic economies of research sites, the indirect discourses through which research subjects speak, constitute simple ways in which affects of our everyday lives can inform research method' (Hickey-Moody 2014, 93). This idea is supported by Finley (2012, 72) who makes the following claim: 'arts-based methodologies bring both arts and social inquiry out of the elitist institutions of academe and art museums, and relocate inquiry within the realm of local, personal, everyday places and events'. Our lived realities and everyday experiences become the research site and research encounter that no longer lurks without but rather within.

Hickey-Moody (2017, 1086) uses affective pedagogy 'to work in exploring aesthetics as a form of communication and art as a way of crafting new affective relationships'. Through art, we are able to do research in a way that is attuned to affect, to response and to doing. 'Critical arts-based research is active, productive; it performs. The emphasis in this type of research is on doing' (Finley 2017, 573). Which leaves us to ponder what inquiry requires of us. It requires us to take action, to be affected, to be aware, to notice, to receive the gifts, to stop, to listen, to create, to perform, to dismantle, to question, to reformulate our questions and, finally, to find that which we have not yet lost.

4.5 A 'Recipe' for Arts-Based Inquiry

So, I opened the gift, the notebook with the blank pages, and I finally wrote something in it. I recorded a 'recipe' of how to cook up an arts-based research encounter. Think of this 'recipe' as the kind that is orally passed down from generation to generation and changed a little bit according to what is the available and what you like. Please use with caution, bravery and joy.

Marguerite's recipe for arts-based inquiry

Ingredients
Materials that can be used to make art. Masking tape is essential.
People, and/or things who are willing to work with you. You can call these your participants.
A recording device, a camera, a notebook, and a drawing pad. Basically, your smartphone.
Questions. Just one question to start out with is OK, but be prepared for your question leading to other questions.
A plan. People will expect you to lead them through the process, so, be prepared with some kind of blueprint or sequence of how things will unfold. This will probably be in your head, but make sure others can follow what is in your head.
Flexibility. Be more concerned with the 'moment' of the engagement than with your blueprint or planned sequence of events. Things will not go as you imagined. In fact, you might have a two-hour workshop in which no one answers the question you posed at the beginning. That's OK. You are learning things. Maybe you need to change the question.
Bravery and willingness to be wrong. You are taking a risk and you need to understand that the outcome will not be what you expected. Masking tape can fix almost everything.
Theory … or something like that. When all is said and done, you need a little something to help you make sense of it all.
Consent forms, inclusivity and kindness. Remember to honour and respect the humans, in all their forms, as well as the more-than-humans that participate. They are meeting you in a research encounter. Without them, it would just be you – asking rhetorical questions.

Method
Take all the ingredients and give it a good stir. As you stir, allow the mixture to help you stay with your predicament. When the consistency becomes aesthetically pleasing, you can serve it.

Tip: If you happen to be an academic and an artist keep the following in mind: 'An intellectual says a simple thing in a hard way. An artist says a hard thing in a simple way.'– Charles Bukowski.[2]

Good luck and have fun!

5

To Not Be Unworthy of What Happens to Us, We Go to the Morgues Ourselves: Wounded Becomings

Do not imitate reality, collaborate with it.
– Bousquet (1979, 28)

5.1 A Silent March

We are wearing black. We are angry. We are sad. We are worried. We are gathering at the main building. The march is about to start. The Steyn statue[1] is awkwardly present. We have been here before. We had seen CR Swart[2] fall. The past is present and the presence of the past is felt. But we are here now. And now we are getting ready for a march to protest gender-based violence.

It is Friday, 6 September 2019, and the university has declared a day of mourning for the victims and survivors of gender-based violence. A messages sent to staff and students the previous day reads:

> The recent rape and murder of 19-year-old Media and Film Studies student at the University of Cape Town (UCT), Uyinene Mrwetyana, and the murder of University of the Western Cape (UWC) student, Jesse Hess, are painful reminders of the pervasive nature of misogyny and patriarchal violence that impedes the freedom of women/womxn in South Africa. The UFS stands in solidarity with UCT and UWC, and all other South African universities that are currently steeped in this national crisis pertaining to gender-based violence.
>
> The UFS perceives this as an enduring manifestation of patriarchy that results in women's/womxn's subordination, inequality, and violation of bodily integrity.

Figure 15 A silent march, 2019.
Photograph, Liezl Dick.

These horrific events underscore the extent to which attempts to address women's/woman's inequality and gender-based violence nationally, and more pertinently at universities, have failed. *Recent discussions have underscored the issue of 'belonging' as a concern in Higher Education contexts. Belonging is often couched in the language of 'access' and 'transformation'. However, these terms often provide limited substantive change for students who experience a sense of marginalisation and alienation at South African universities.* Decolonisation discourse challenges the nature of hegemonic knowledge production that excludes voices of alterity.

Epistemic violence is central to decolonisation discourse referring to the nature of hegemonic knowledge production that excludes voices of alterity. *The extent to which knowledge production manifests in universities is, however, not only white and Western, but also male and masculine.* South African universities are therefore confronted again with the urgency of recognising and responding to the issue of women's/womxn's subordination, with specific emphasis on their safety and freedom (emphasis added). (Petersen 2019)

As we walk in silence, we see the faces of many colleagues and students. A sea of solemn eyes, bodies dressed in black. Then we start to sing, Izono Zethu (our only sin is being female). Up ahead, we see our colleagues Lebo, Deidre, Karabo and Nomsa. They are moving together along with the crowd. Walking through their own story, through this chapter. A few days later, we have lunch together. We talk and draw and write and listen. We ask, 'Please share your story. How did you get here? What was your journey? What does it mean to be an educator in this space?'

5.2 The Wound as Event

In this chapter, we will be exploring affective incidents in the professional and personal journeys of four educators at the UFS. We will be reading the narratives through the lens of Deleuze's concept of the event, or, more specifically, the wound as event, to highlight the interrelatedness of the lives, experiences, intensities, social and political forces, affects and becomings of those who are part of a process of transformation. Here, we will see the value of Deleuze's philosophy and concepts for making sense and living in a rapidly changing society. The event, 'as part of the Deleuzian "and" of becoming, the molecular thresholds of bodies and things as events are described by Deleuze in terms of affective happenings; occasions where things and bodies are altered' (Colman 2010, 13).

Deleuze is not interested in the fixed, static nature of reality; he is interested in the processual nature of things, subjectivity and life. Deleuze is hence not concerned with the outcomes of events but more about the 'characteristics governing the effect of events. We cannot be sure of the outcomes of events, but we can describe where and how they have reverberated' (Williams 2008, 6). Consequently, his theory and way of interrogating the world privileges processes and change to fixed identity and certainty. He tunes in to flux and flow, and prefers to favour movement rather than to fixate on certainty or universal 'truths'. By implication, such an approach to life is not aimed at predictions about the future. No, Deleuze's processual ontology and univocity of being want to plug into the change, movement and flux of our changing world, to allow for an intensive experience of what is happening to us and the world around us.

As mentioned before (Section 1.4.1), we perceive subjectivity to be a by-product of affective and intensive processes and events. In the words of James Williams (2008, 129): 'Conscious persons exist against a background of unconscious and impersonal events standing as the conditions for any identity.' Such an understanding of subjectivity is helpful when we talk about social change and transformation, as it gives us the tools for taking a closer look at the (political, social, material and affective) forces and flows that shape educator subjectivities. Furthermore, it enables us to take a closer look at the becomings (how they were shaped/influenced by past experiences, both personal and professional) of these educators and its entanglement with their lived experiences, while also shedding light on how the expectations of educators about the future might shape their lives in the here and now.

For the analysis of our chapter, it is important to mention that all these processual events and flows are connected (Williams 2011, 81) – it forms an interconnected web of pre-individual relations/interactions. Events refer to many processes that play out simultaneously. Here, we get a glimpse of what Deleuze means when he refers to our ontological interrelatedness and a concomitant ethics of relationality – we are constituted in and through relations, events and processes. The event is not something that only happens in the conscious minds of individuals but 'rather a set of multiple interactions running through bodies, ideal structures ... and virtual structures' (Williams 2008, 2).

Identity, then, 'is a cloak thrown over many processes such that each is an indivisible becoming, a duration, modes nothing but modes, such that they all enter into harmony through shared vibrations. A chair, anything whatsoever, is an event as the harmony of multiple processes of becoming' (Williams 2011, 83).

When events resonate through institutions, people and communities, transformations occur (Williams 2008, 2).

Very often, transformation and change are triggered by specific incidents, or what we will call affective incidents or accidents. Such an incident might be emotionally loaded and physically intense and resonate through the individual, the network of interactions with others and things and, consequently, also through institutions. This incident befalling us can be perceived of as a wound 'because each event is "incarnated" by the physical series as something that comes from the outside and forces us to change. This physical event occurs as an intense and urgent concentration of the past and of the future in the present' (Williams 2011, 86).

For technical purposes, it is important to mention that the incident is not (all of) the wound – the wound is not an empirical event. The incident must happen, however, for the event to occur. The incident becomes the wound-event when we counter-actualize, or work with, what happens to us. In this sense, the wound-event does not flow from one single cause, but rather, resonates with incidents in the past and in the future. Rather than a cause, the wound-event turns into an endeavour of becoming. Deleuze plays with an understanding of causality that does not adhere to our common-sense thinking regarding cause and effect (Reynolds 2007, 57). The incident has the potential to disrupt and alter, not only the flows and intensities shaping our future trajectories (i.e. how we see and imagine the world, and who we are becoming) but also our understanding of past experiences. Ultimately, the affective incident, if embraced and worked with or counter-actualized, in the words of Deleuze, can help us to understand ourselves differently, and what is happening to us from multiple perspectives, some more common sense in nature than others (Lawlor 2019, 10).

It is helpful to be reminded at this stage that Deleuze is not a big fan of what? questions. His affinity for processes and becomings make the how? why? and who? questions more relevant for his processual ontology (Williams 2008). The question is thus not, what happened? It is, instead, why did the thing that happened change us? Who were changed by the thing that happened? And, ultimately, in this chapter, we ask, how do we respond to the wound-event and *become worthy of what happens to us?*

For the purposes of this chapter, it is also valuable to highlight how wounding can become an artistic event. Deleuze refers to the work of French novelist Joë Bousquet, who sustained a spinal cord injury in the First World War that left him paralysed. Deleuze uses Bousquet as an example of someone who did not deny or resent the accident and consequential event – the shot fired at him. Instead of resentment, Bousquet embraced the wound, by returning to the incident in his books, and creating and reliving the experience as a former and future self, which resulted in the merging of selves and multiplicities (Williams 2008, 155). The wound, counter-actualized and transformed, becomes an artistic and physical event 'and the life as an artist of acute sensibility and great passion rises out of, or hovers with, the curtailed life spent bedridden in deep pain and protected behind a heavy curtain from direct light' (Williams 2008, 155). Through his creative writing, Bousquet strived to become worthy of what had happened to him. His creations and creativity can never undo or refute what had happened to him, but his writings can put his wounding 'in touch with a source of value running counter to its suffering and injuries' (Williams 2008, 155). Through the creative act, the past wound, the future wound and the present suffering alter the 'intensity of relations between these different times of the event'. Through this creative endeavour, our understanding and experience of the past and the future will change; by embracing the event/accident, a potentially devastating occurrence is transformed and gives birth to compassion and acceptance (Williams 2008, 155). 'For Deleuze', writes Janz (2019, 63), 'the event is tied to the sense of things, in Deleuze's meaning of the term. "Sense" refers to the point at which language and the world meet. Speaking, writing and performing create events in the world'. And this is the value of the creative act of counter-actualization for the purposes of our book: to tell our stories, retell and draw them, becoming with our stories by sharing them, becoming by listening to the stories of others, generating a myriad of different views on what happened to us. In this sense, 'we are but transformers of flows of intensity into novel flows' (Williams 2008, 157). Deleuze's concept of the wound-event helps us to shed light on the complex and interrelated nature of the processes of subjectification and the by-products of these processes that we come to know as educator subjectivities.

So, how can Deleuze's concept of the event, and the wound as event, help us to tell the story of four women who work in the education space during a time of social change?

5.3 Collective Biographical Storying

In this chapter, we employ a collective biographical style of writing, in which contradictions in narratives are considered productive, and of more value than coherence or 'truth'. As a feminist methodology, collective biography highlights the embodied memories and experiences of the female participants and the situatedness of our knowledge production. Consequently, we embraced the partiality, subjectiveness and relationality of knowledge that was created and shared during this session, while also rethinking ontology and subjectivity formation as affective (Gannon and Gonick 2019; Pullen, Rhodes and Thanem 2017, 117). We followed the everyday lives of four women who work in the education space and explored how they were trying to make sense of their realities, relationships, occupations and selves in a world that doesn't always work in their favour, or accommodate them or in which they don't feel at home. The chapter forms a collective affective assemblage, for which we used feminist methodology to create a safe space and a place of belonging for these uncomfortable experiences that can't be digested by the organization/system. In this sense, we wanted to comprehend and navigate our ontological entanglements and communal becomings – our lives as events – while also highlighting the contradictions in our narratives; how are we complicit in keeping this unjust system in place? (Gannon and Gonick 2019; Pullen et al. 2017, 117).

Consequently, we worked with the affective incidents that resonated and moved us, the researchers, as we listened and participated in the narratives that emerged in the research encounter. We had to listen to the affects and intensities of our bodies, and we allowed these to affect us in the process of writing this chapter. The memories of the participants connected with and affected our own memories; we embarked on an 'experimental, emergent and engaging' endeavour, 'where thought and being were not separate' (Davies and Gannon 2012, 373). Therefore, 'what becomes knowable in this process is the entangled enlivening of being' (Davies and Gannon 2012, 373).

We used drawing as a method of narrative elicitation as well as interpretation. Liezl guided the participants through a process of drawing and telling their stories, while Marguerite listened and made interpretative drawings while the participants were speaking. The end result was a rhizomatic drawing of criss-crossing narratives that emerged during the focus group session. We used the drawings made by the participants and the oral narrations, together with the interpretive 'story map' that Marguerite had made, to connect the different biographical narratives into one story of educator subjectivity during a time of social change. In doing this, we experimented with a form of analysis or interpretation that did not take place after the research encounter but emerged during the research encounter. The 'data' and 'data interpretation' thus emerged simultaneously to form a knowledge exchange between researchers and participants, in which the final narrative could be negotiated and changed in a responsive process. The narrative that emerged will be presented in the following section.

5.4 A Story of Four Women

5.4.1 Setting the Scene

Book: The women are sitting in the boardroom of the Free State Centre for Human Rights. They eat cold sausages, meatballs and spinach quiche, while talking about the significant incidents that changed them as educators – those incidents that made them think differently about who they are, about what they are doing and why they are here in the first place. Six women in the room, sharing their life stories. Marguerite is making interpretive drawings on a big piece of paper as they speak. She is trying to capture and respond to the affects and intensities as they are being conveyed, in the moment, immanently and immediately. We are experimenting with methods. Liezl is asking the questions and she is nervous about how little time we have to engage with the four participants. How do you capture a life in one hour? However, they've known each other for several years and through difficult times, and the 'focus group' turns into a comfortable space of sharing that is permeated with sadness and strength. Reading their narratives through the lens of the wound-event is challenging; Deleuze prefers to focus on the pre-individual intensities and flows of processes of subjectification and, hence, our radical relationality that precedes individual notions of identity and fixity. And this is helpful, because, in this way, the researchers can attempt to understand *how* educators become who they are, and how educators' subjectivities are the results of bigger and smaller processes, flows, intensities and affects. In other words, it opens up the possibility of thinking differently, processually and authentically, about how educators become who they are. Guided by these theoretical underpinnings, the reader is now invited to go on a journey with these participants. Can you identify the intensities and flows in their narratives that made them who they are? Can you identify the affective incidents that sparked events? How did they counter-actualize these events? How are political, social and economic events intertwined with smaller flows of affect and intensity? How do they talk about the future, and how does this influence the present? Are there virtual becomings, potentialities and flows that are actualized by their narratives? I can give you some clues. Take note of the affective sections in the narratives (in italics), of the events that reverberated through their lives in these instances and, most of all, how they responded to these experiences.

5.4.2 Out of the Misfortune, Happiness Bloomed

Lebo was a happy child, who grew up with her parents and three sisters in a community in Bloemfontein. As a teenager, she experienced loneliness for the first time, as she had to change schools often. But life improved for her and she eventually made friends. *In the second year of her university studies, her parents were retrenched. She had to halt her studies and had to find a job.*

> This was an extremely difficult time in my life. But I turned into this career woman, made lots of friends and had a baby. Out of the misfortune happiness bloomed.

Figure 16 Four women, 2019.
Pencil drawing, Artist: Marguerite Müller.

She enjoyed being a parent and felt confident about career prospects.

> *But then I lost my partner when my daughter was five years old.* It was devastating. For a while I couldn't pick myself up.

Once again, however, she had to pull herself together after a tragic loss and had to continue with her career and raising her child.

> This bridge on my drawing indicates that period of time. *It was a time of change and transition.* Now I am okay. I am in a good space with regards to work and my personal life.

Nomsa is the last-born in a family of six girls.

I was a quiet and sweet girl, they say. They could leave me on my own for hours.

Her family dynamics were complicated. Her mother was a domestic worker.

She stayed with the family she worked for, and hence never lived with us. So, until today, I call my older sister, Mama. She is just six years older than me.

Book: Keep in mind, apartheid and colonization can be viewed as events that started long before Nomsa's childhood and have effects that will resonate through bodies, family dynamics and institutions for decades to come.

Nomsa's family dynamics also complicated her education and school years.

I first went to a Zulu school, then to a Sotho school and then to a Tswana school. For my high school years I attended a boarding school. *Schools were very far from home, because during apartheid there were no schools close to my home.* So, when you go to a boarding school it was an achievement. *Although my mother was a domestic worker, she made sure we all went to good schools.* It was a prestigious thing. And when we went home during the holidays, we were the centre of attention.

After school, Nomsa studied nursing, but she did not enjoy the course.

If your parents weren't rich you couldn't study what you wanted to.

She studied at UFS and eventually obtained her PhD.

So, although I started out as a nurse, studying something I really did not want to, in the process I became a researcher, lecturer and residence head.

Deidre comes from a culturally diverse family,

a mixed masala of everything. I always tell my friends I am so lucky, because I get to celebrate so many holidays: Christmas, Eid, you name it. And this is why I am so passionate about breaking away from stereotypical notions; *where I come from, we are all so different, but can embrace each other's differences.*

Deidre finished school when she was sixteen.

My mother's biggest fear was that I would *fall pregnant* and it was frowned upon, especially if you were Muslim. But I was a very docile child and never went anywhere.

After finishing her studies, she was appointed as a residence manager.

I immediately loved the job and liked working with the students.

While working at the university, Deidre had her own daughter.

> It was difficult to juggle the job, and the baby. Then, two months ago, *I had a miscarriage. I am still busy processing that.* I am sharing this with all of you now because this is what we are doing now – sharing. I am okay, but *it is a process.*

Karabo doesn't remember much about her childhood:

> In my picture the sun symbolizes my birth; a new dawn arrived when I was born. I like hyping myself up. *When my father lost his job, and all hell broke loose. He became abusive*, but not against me. He would put me outside and then *beat up my mom and sisters inside*.

Karabo didn't trust anyone because of her abusive father.

> *I started to have imaginary friends*, and I learned that life can be better if I surround myself with them. I had a lot of imaginary boyfriends too.

When Karabo came to the UFS, she created a bubble around herself.

> I didn't register what happened to me at home. I was in my bubble. *I remember my grandmother told my mother I should go to the psychiatric ward because I spoke to Sarah, my imaginary friend all the time.* But my mom, luckily, refused.

Eventually, Karabo's mother got a court interdict against the father, and he had to leave their family house.

> But he took everything in the house. Teaspoons, cutlery, beds. *We had to sleep on the floor for six months.* So, because of this, I will never ever be dependent on a man. I don't care what happens. That's where my independence grew from.

Karabo went on to study law and her life improved. She is passionate about law. She took on leadership positions. Eventually, she took the residence head job, which gave her financial stability.

> Now I had a job, but *this was also when the 'black tax' started*. Because I earned an income, my direct and extended family expected me to provide for them. This is how it works with black families. It's rough. It hit me pretty hard. *You never understand it until you are in it. Like motherhood. And love.* But I coped with that. I also met the husband here, Mr Zimbabwe. Ja, I am a feminist at heart, but when I go to Zimbabwe I kneel for men, I do what I have to do because I love him.
>
> **Book:** The narratives of the six women become entangled in the space of the boardroom. How did their childhood experiences shape their professional

identities? By sharing their personal histories and narratives, something opened up between them, and a deeper sharing and becoming-together became possible.

5.4.3 Unforgotten Wounds

The narratives hover in the air of the seminar room. Liezl looks at their drawings while trying to process the information and emotions evoked by the shared stories. Something catches her eye on Karabo's drawing; there is a blue and brown stick figure with a long neck, resembling an almost-disembodied head. Karabo had drawn her head as separate, disembodied from the body, only connected with a thin line. The picture indicates a shift from a former, happier period in her childhood, to a clearly disruptive phase, when her father's abusive behaviour started. The face of the stick figure is solemn, without expression, while the body is in distress. The stick figure doesn't have arms or legs. Maybe did she feel disempowered in that space? The drawing makes Liezl wonder if Karabo had to learn from a young age to disconnect her mind/head from her body, while also having to create a safe imaginary space for herself, removed from her immediate reality. Liezl pictures her as a little girl, sitting in the TV room of their family's house, in front of the television, desperately trying to escape from the overwhelming reality of abuse. She escapes into an imaginary world filled with friends and comfort. She found her solace in imaginary friends and tried to forget about her abusive father while she slept on the floor, and all their suffering. However, if memories are embodied knowledge (Cixous and Calle-Gruber 1997) and 'stored a language on the deep surfaces in/on the body' (Davies et al. 2005, 344), does the body ever really forget?

> Fear of traces, fear of memory: it is clearly a fear in the present. We are always afraid of seeing ourselves suffer. It is like when we have an open wound: we are terribly afraid of looking at it … and at the same time we are perhaps the one person capable of looking at it. What do we fear? (Cixous and Calle-Gruber 1997, 25).

Braidotti agrees: '[the] enfleshed Deleuzian subject … is a folding in of external influences and a simultaneously unfolding outwards of affects. A mobile entity, an enfleshed sort of memory that repeats. The Deleuzian body is ultimately an embodied memory' (2000, 159).

In this boardroom today, Karabo's body is not forgetting. She bravely faces the wounds of her unhappy childhood and life, as all the others did too: Nomsa, growing up without a mother; Lebo, losing a partner; Deidre, going through the pain of a miscarriage. We are all sharing these affects of pain and suffering. We all have our wounds. Or do the wounds have us? We form an affective assemblage where our narratives, emotions and embodied memories are folded into one another, enfolded by the space of the room and the campus. While we share our stories, the interrelatedness of our wound-events became clear and in the intimate space of the boardroom we counter-actualize our wounds, our affective incidents and our traumas by sharing them with one another. We allowed our pain, our trauma, but also our joy, to reverberate through each other's stories and lives.

> **Book:** I look down at these six brave women. In the infinity of my mind's eye, I can see all the events that brought them together, to this room, and I can also see into the future, the events and incidents that will still happen and shape and intertwine their lives. There is one specific incident that affected all of them in some way or another. It would be wrong to say that some traumas are bigger than others. But, dare I say, some events reverberate more intensely through bodies than others. I am referring to what came to be known as the Reitz incident, which happened in 2007/2008 on the UFS Bloemfontein campus. The incident refers to a 10-minute video that was posted on YouTube on 28 February 2008, which was made in reaction to the policy of racial integration of residences of the UFS. At that stage, campus residences were segregated by race. The new placement policy aimed to enhance and speed up the racial integration process. It was, after all, 2007, thirteen years after apartheid laws and policies had been abolished. In the video, four white male students 'initiate' five black cleaners, by taking them through a series of notorious and humiliating initiation rituals. Posting the video on YouTube had far-reaching repercussions for the UFS management and for higher education institutions in South Africa, in general. The incident made it clear that racism is still a structural and pervasive issue in higher education institutions (Lazenby and Radebe 2011; Marais and De Wet 2009). The incident caused huge upheaval on the Bloemfontein campus and racial tension was rife. Students protested on the 'Red Square' where the Steyn statue used to stand (Section 5.1). Consequences are still reverberating through the community to this day. The Reitz incident can be read as the manifestation of the apartheid/colonization wound-event; an incident that set a process of rapid transformation at the UFS on track. 'When events resonate through institutions', Williams writes, 'people and communities, transformations occur' (2008, 2).

> **Lebo:** *The Reitz incident and the aftermath was intense.* The placement policy was still new and there was a lot of tension among the students. *The white student leaders didn't want to adhere to the placement policy,*

while the black student leaders were in favour of its implementation. We had long discussions with them, but they were very much opposed to this progressive, transformative and necessary placement policy. The white leaders decided to stage a peaceful protest against the policy by camping in front of the main building. I and other residence heads convened on the Madelief *stoep* with a bottle of wine, just discussing what was happening on campus and supporting each other. *I had my first real confrontation of what racial tension is on this campus.* One night I was driving to my residence, *and I was driving behind a pickup truck with white students. They would stop in the middle of the street, throw a tyre in the street and set it alight. Then they would drive on and a couple of meters further they would repeat this exercise.* In the morning, all the boom gates at the entrances to campus were broken and fires were ignited on campus. The next morning, the dean called us in, demanding answers, saying we should know what's going on, seeing that we live on campus and insinuating that this was the work of black students. '*Most black students don't own cars, Sir, never mind pickup trucks*', an upset male colleague of mine told the dean. *You know, it is really difficult to understand myself in this context.* All the residence head meetings were conducted in Afrikaans. I didn't understand what they were talking about. So I could leave this space, or I could learn Afrikaans. I decided to take Afrikaans classes. I never thought I would be here for more than ten years. I managed to pick myself up personally, after the death of my partner, and professionally, even through all these protests and challenges. I just *had* to. I was really down at times, but I just had to go on. *So, when the #fallist movement started and the 2015/2016 protests took place, I knew I had to decide how to position myself.*

Liezl: Lebo's story reminds me of the endurance we need when we find ourselves in a transformative context. The limits of the body and psyche are really pushed when you find yourself in a space and time of rapid social change. It really challenges the mental health of many educators and students.

Deidre: Something in the space that I was not aware of before, was the *psychological issues of students*. I had this one student studying accounting. She was brilliant, got 90 percent for all her subjects. She caused havoc in the residence, drawing little rats everywhere and calling herself Raticia. *When I confronted her, she told me she wanted to be a rat.* Why on earth, I asked, a rat? Because rats are intelligent and manipulative and they can outsmart humans, she said. I was blown away. *Then she tried to start a cult in her class and frightened the whole res [residence] with talk of demons.* We took her to a psychiatrist and took her to the mental hospital. To this day, I still struggle to understand what happened to her. She had no support from her family. *Her mom told me she is not their problem anymore. One night, the student tried to commit suicide.* I called the mother, but she said she has visitors and she is in Cape Town, which is 1,000 km from Bloemfontein; what is she supposed to do? This poor girl had absolutely no support from her family and*, institutionally, it felt like the support for an extreme situation like this was lacking.*

Liezl: Most people will never really understand the extreme challenges a residence manager has to deal with. Mostly, this job is looked down upon, as a low-level, support staff position. Only those who were once residence managers will understand the 24/7, all-consuming nature of this work. It challenges you at all levels imaginable: psychologically, politically, emotionally and professionally. To this day, it remains the most fulfilling, but the most challenging job I have ever done. I had to learn and grow, I had to transform and change. But when Deidre shared the following story, all of us residence managers in the room were shaken to the core.

Deidre: So, this is an incident that took place while I was pregnant with my daughter. One of my students was pregnant too and *she went into premature labour*, and the parents told me, sorry they are in Oudtshoorn, so I must deal with it. And, so, *I had to go with her to the hospital every day* and she didn't have anything, so I had to buy her bottles and stuff, *but I was pregnant myself.* After the birth, I was going to the hospital every day for six hours to make sure the feedings went well. *Unfortunately, this girl just eventually distanced herself from the baby. The hospital called me one Friday night and she was nowhere to be found.* I went to the hospital and they told me *she had left the baby behind and the baby was in distress.* At one o'clock in the morning I was looking for her, but couldn't find her anywhere. We phoned the parents and the mother said they are too far away, they don't even have money to come there, so *I had to deal with it. I felt like I had no support. I had to do it all by myself.* In the morning, they called and said the girl was out clubbing, and I drove to the hospital and *when I arrived, the staff told me the baby had passed away.* So, the hospital staff told me *I have to go to the morgue now* and *I must go and identify the baby*. And I said, wait a moment, *this is now a bit too much for me.* I phoned around and asked for help, *but nobody could help me*. And then something happened that *really traumatized me: In the morgue, the babies were vacuum-packed, like pieces of meat, and the nurse picked them up like they were files*! Asking me, *is it this one, or is it this one?* And all of this happened while *I was pregnant with my own child*. So, I think *what we have to deal with as residence heads is a lot more than anybody not working in this space can imagine*. I don't think anybody *understands the intensity of our work*. So, I asked myself, *what do I have to do in this space to support these kids* and *how far do you really have to go to help them, before you have a mental breakdown yourself?*

Book: According to Deleuze (1990, 149), "the event is not what occurs (an accident); it is rather inside what occurs, the purely expressed. It signals and awaits us ... it is what must be understood, willed and represented in that which occurs. Bousquet goes on to say, 'Become the man of your misfortunes; learn to embody their perfection and brilliance.' Nothing more can be said, and no more has ever been said: to become worthy of what happens to us, and thus to will and release the event, to become the offspring of one's own events, and thereby to be reborn, to have one more birth'.

5.4.4 How Far Do We Really Need to Go?

Book: Where is the line and where does my duty begin and end? As Deidre's story unfolded, the everyday, ordinary experiences became grotesque; the mundane triggered existential questions, psychological angst caused trauma that lingers for years. How much can a body endure? There are so many dimensions and layers to Deidre's story of what it means to be a woman, a mother, a body, and what it means to be a residence head and how the personal and professional are conflated in this pedagogical positioning.

Liezl: What I find interesting in Deidre's narrative is how the university system is seemingly unable to adapt to the lived experiences of the student and the traumatized educator. The university system is not geared to provide sufficient support to the educator who actually manages to conflate the personal and the professional that goes beyond the call of duty. A disconnect exists between the university's formal structures and the lived realities of students and staff. The system can't stomach or digest Deidre's request for support. The system wants to compute the problem it faces in terms of numbers, digits, data and, hence, the quantifiable; but can't make sense of the complexity it is confronted with. It spits out a fault message, 'Error!: deal with this problem by yourself.' So, this is exactly what we do: We go to the morgue ourselves, deal with the unimaginable act of identifying the corpse of a baby, while still being pregnant ourselves. We soldier on like so many women have done in this country and will do for decades to come.

Book: Living with their woundedness in this broken reality: Where are they now in terms of transformation? Those who live through times of social change might never be able to answer this question. If only it was possible to provide them with the different temporal perspectives that I have; subsisting in empty time, it is possible for me to see far into the past and into the future. But no, these women have to live the questions themselves. (Rilke 2011)

Liezl: We have reached the end of our focus group; our time is up, but I have one last question for the participants. Something that I think about quite often: Where we are now in terms of transformation? Where are we going from here? If you had to draw a trajectory of your life and a trajectory of the transformation of the university space, what would these look like? And what do we foresee for the future? Can we imagine a future transformed? Or not? What would the ideal future situation look like for all of us?

Karabo: To know where I am going, I need to know where it started. What is expected from myself in the space, expected from me as an employee, *not* from Karabo the individual, but what is expected from me in my role as educator so that I can align myself with the project. I want to align with visions and missions of the transformation project, and moving forward I want to deliver a service that empowers. I want to make a contribution where things are working irrespective of my presence. I want to create a sustainable, functional community that is self-sufficient. It's the only way transformation will work. It makes me think of Nelson Mandela. People thought South Africa would not work after he was gone and that is what happens when you attach success to a certain person. It's not only the person, the leader, that matters. Yes, that too, but it's the people that contribute, build and sustain change. So, that is how I foresee transformation and change manifesting. Transformation will only work when you don't attach successes to a specific person. The system needs to be sustainable in itself, and for that to happen, people need to be empowered and sustainable in themselves.

Liezl: Deidre was frustrated with students and their demanding attitudes. She is opposed to a system that infantilizes students, a system that feeds into their demands and needs without empowering them to take on the adult world out there. For her, being an educator requires a fine balance between looking after yourself and meeting the needs of the students. In the in-between space, where these educators are working, this is a particularly difficult balance to strike as the educator almost always finds herself in the *liminal space of becoming educator/becoming other; always already on the threshold of the personal and the professional.*

Deidre: So, how far do you go when doing this job and how much of yourself do you give? *A difficult lesson I had to learn was how to set boundaries.* This generation of students is very different from the previous generation. They definitely have a greater sense of entitlement. We, as educators, hence, need strong boundaries while empowering them at the same time. We have to guard against micromanaging them by doing everything for them.

Book: Deidre's feedback seemed to trigger Nomsa.

Nomsa: At the moment, I am in a space where I think *the blame game should stop*, especially blaming students. We should stop blaming the students. There is a certain reality these students are facing, and each different space and each changing phase has its own reality. And the reality is that students have different capabilities and advantages. We have students whose priority is their families back home, students who have to pay the so-called 'black tax' by providing food and money to their families back at home. This is what the students have to do with their bursary money meant for books. This is the harsh reality of our social space. So, when you say students have to be less demanding or more mature, it's not going to happen. *We, as educators and the university community, have to realize that the reality and the world are not perfect.* We will never get perfect students and the space will never be perfect. The question we rather have to ask ourselves is, *what can we do with this broken reality that we have to deal with every day?* Blaming students won't get us anywhere. Some of the challenges they are facing because of their problematic school background are very real. *They come from poor, disadvantaged backgrounds, and this affects how they engage with their studies and the world around them. Their social context or family life is overwhelming for them too.* The reality in this country is harsh, and this is where the students come from. But we have to ask, how do we nurture the students in the reality we find ourselves in? I am here for the students, and if I am not giving the students hope, and if I am not going to be the person the students can see hope in, I would rather not be here. And it frustrates me when my colleagues are always seeing students as a problem, as a challenge and not taking the reality of the students life into account. They can't see the perspective of the students. We will continue to struggle with student retention and pass rates if we don't take their reality and backgrounds into account. *If we don't see the students as products of a specific social system where this system has some definite problems and challenges, all our efforts as educators will never be effective.*

Liezl: Nomsa is upset. This is something she feels very strongly about. Our time has run out. The boardroom space is filled with warmth and intensity. Marguerite shows us the drawings she made while listening to the narratives.

Marguerite: The stories you shared are *precious and beautiful*, while also *valuable and terrible*. Thank you very much for sharing. The purpose of our project is to share stories and experiences with one another. *And listening to your stories made me think differently about this space*. We have known each other for so long, yet we know very little of what each of us have lived through. And this is apt, *as the research we are doing is focused on the transformation of ourselves too*. This whole human assemblage is so complex. This focus group made it possible for me to think of *this space as a complex, entangled space, where narratives form an affective assemblage and interrelated events*. So, while you were talking, I kept *responding by drawing your narratives, and focused on the things that jumped out for me*. I know this drawing will probably only make sense to me, as it represents layers and layers of *affects depicting affective incidents and becomings*. The black pen indicates pain and suffering, while the orange pen is the hopeful experiences and affects. As you can see, *hope and despair, good and difficult times, become wrapped up into each other*.

Book:

When acting one role, the actor is always acting out other roles. The role has the same relation to the actor as the future and past have to the instantaneous present, which corresponds to them on the line of the Aion. The actor thus actualizes the event, but in a way that is entirely different from the actualization of the event in the depth of things. Or rather, the actor redoubles this cosmic or physical actualization in their own way, which is singularly superficial but because of it, more distinct, trenchant and pure. Thus, the actor delimits the original, disengages from it an abstract line and keeps from the event only its contour and its splendor, becoming thereby the actor of one's own events – a *counter-actualization* (Deleuze 1990, 150).

Figure 17 How we got here, 2019.
Focus group participant drawings.

5.5 Conclusion: Our Suffering Becomes Our Growth, Our Wound Is Our Becoming

In this chapter, we used collective biography, narratives, an affective assemblage and the wound-events as tools to understand how educators' subjectivities are produced by experiences and affective incidents. By sharing experiences, drawing life stories and listening to one another, we, as educators, could rework and counter-actualize the traumatic events that had shaped us. In this chapter, it became clear that the professional and the personal identity binary can no longer hold. In a space of transformation and rapid change, all events are interrelated and we are becoming-other and becoming educators because of these shared events.

The educators/residence managers shared their personal stories, and this created a trusted environment where the challenges of their personal and professional experiences could be shared. The events of their lives did not discern between what was personal and what was of a professional nature; all experiences affect the educator. In turn, educators affect one another and are affected by their environment, by students and by the past memories and future expectations.

To be worthy of what happens to us, the event and the transformation occurring in ourselves and our world must be embraced (Williams 2008, 81). Why? Because a refusal to embrace the change and transformation will prevent becoming and will deny the processual and changing nature of life and reality. We have to keep up with the movement, stay in touch with events and flow with the flux, to ensure we are worthy of what happens to us and, consequently, change with the transforming world around us (Williams 2008, 81). Resenting the incident and consequential event will, thus, stifle becoming. Consequently, it will be beneficial to avoid fixating on the traumatic incident and resenting what happened, or blaming others; instead we should work with something that takes place *within* the experience, counter-actualize that which is actually happening by actively deciding to work with it and open up the possible consequences (read: new interpretations of cause and effect) for us. To be worthy of the event, we have to try and grasp what happens to us from a multiplicity of perspectives, which is made possible by a state of mind, intuition or attitude that perceives our incident from the viewpoint of infinity, empty time (Aion). By exploring the different, possible perspectives on what happens to us, we care for our experiences – we do not accept the obvious, easy and taken-for-granted answers. No, instead, we care for our experiences by exploring the multitude of possible meanings it can entail. There is no 'right' answer but only a multiplicity of questions (Lawlor 2019, 19–20; Williams 2008, 13). 'If events are wounds then … In order to be an event a wound must be worked through creatively in an individuating path, that is change and be changed by the path' (Williams 2008, 12).

The counter-actualization Deleuze writes about refers to what we are trying to do to make sense of our changing lives in a time of rapid social change: negotiating the past, imagining the future, doing the writing itself in the present moment, but the being and becoming in another time that is not chronological or linear. To write, for us, the authors, is to counter-actualize, to make sense of our past experiences and use them to create better futures – not only for ourselves, but for others too. Subjectivity is relational, and our acts and events are intertwined. While writing, we constantly delve into memories to make sense of experiences, while also projecting certain expectations about the future.

5.6 Drawing as Analysis

Figure 18 Analysis drawing, 2019.
Pen and highlighter on paper, Marguerite Müller.

In the focus group that informed this chapter, we used drawing as both inquiry and interpretation. Drawing thus helped us understand and shape the narrative. We followed these steps:

1. We invited the participants to draw their life stories.
2. We asked them to share these stories with each another. While they were sharing, Marguerite made an interpretive drawing of their narratives. This visual portrayal of the entanglement of events became part of the interpretive process.
3. We used the drawing interpretation to revisit and connect the narratives of becoming.
4. Finally, we used the drawing to create a new narrative, to show the conflation of the professional/personal binary.

6

Can You Please Come Back Later? A Cartography of Becoming Educators

6.1 Cartographies of Becoming Educators during a Time of Social Change

In this chapter, we will present a cartography of becoming educators during a time of social change. We do this through an engagement with the narrative experiences of people who had recently transitioned from the role of being a student to that of becoming educator. We were thus interested in the process of becoming an educator, and in the interplay between student and educator subjectivities in the context of social change. By using cartography as a methodology, we explored the conflation of theory and methodology to help us explore educator subjectivity further. Cartography allows multiple topics, such as social justice, educator praxis and social change, to be explored and discussed. We hoped that this exploration would help us to develop innovative ways to creatively think through educator subjectivity during social change and transformation.

In this cartography, a number of narrative lines meet. The lines form a rhizome, a map, a net, a nest or a web. At the intersections, we find stories about how we came to be what we are becoming (McAdams and McLean 2013, 234). These intersections form the knots or the nodes, the entanglement of lines, narratives and multiplicities that makes connection and becoming possible. The entanglement of narrative lines forms nodes or multiplicities that make a becoming together, or 'togethering', possible (Ingold 2010). Here, we have a narrative with no beginning and no end, and there are many entryways into it (Masny 2013). Masny makes a distinction between tracing and mapping and says that 'cartographies relate to mappings and mappings relate to the rhizome. Cartographies are captured through the rhizome' (2013, 3). Masny (2013) quotes Deleuze and Guattari (2008, 12) to emphasize that 'tracing and maps are not a dualism; rather, the relationship of the tracing and the map refers to paradoxical forces at work together in an assemblage'. Tree or root structures exist in rhizomes; conversely, a tree branch or root division may begin to burgeon into a rhizome (Deleuze and Guattari 2008, 15). Deleuze and Guattari define a rhizome as an underground root system, an open, decentralized network, which branches out to all sides, unpredictably and horizontally, according to principles that make multiple entryways, multiplicity, connection, a-signifying ruptures and cartography possible (Loots, Coppens, and Sermijn 2017, 111). So, in this chapter, we will think of each narrative as a tree that forms part of a larger rhizome, and we are interested in how a method of mapping and cartography can help us 'enter' into an engagement with educator subjectivity and becoming.

Let me put it differently. I have a four-year-old daughter and one of her favourite books is *Big Bug Log* (Crow and Braun 2016). It is a simple story about a little bug, Bugsy, who goes on a journey to visit his grandmother. Each page has a number of little hidden doors, and as you read the story about Bugsy's journey, there are clues about which door will lead you to the next page. Behind the correct door, you will find a hole in the cardboard book page that leads to the next page. Each page is a story in itself, and Bugsy travels in and through different story pages to eventually reach his grandmother's house. This made me think of a narrative as something that has many holes (or doors) in it, and each hole leads to something else. In our narrative of becoming educators, there are so many points of entry, but, unlike the story of Bugsy, where every page has only one 'right' door leading to the next page, the following story has many doors (or holes) and they lead nowhere in particular. The story we will tell in this chapter is not a linear story with a beginning or an end. It is a story with many holes in it and through these holes the lines of different narratives criss-cross to create a rhizomatic map or cartography.

6.2 A Story with Many Holes and Many Lines

6.2.1 A Dandelion

> I walk across the empty field
> to find a dandelion
> next to the barbed wire fence of Shimla Park
> make a wish, I think
> as the little seeds scatter
> in the winter sun

Figure 19 Dandelion, 2019.
Photograph, Marguerite Müller.

6.2.2 Nowadays

> **Liezl:** Here is a map of our campus. Please point to a place on the map that has significance to your narrative of being a student and becoming an educator. An entry point into your narrative…

Lizzy points to Shimla Park.

> **Lizzy:** A few years ago, when Shimla Park happened, we were students… But nowadays, the students are different. Nowadays the students are rude; they are not able to stand together to fight a cause. They listen selectively. They only listen to what they want to hear. They only listen to attack. They listen [in order] to reply. The students we get now

Figure 20 A map of the UFS campus, 2019.

> are very different from a few years back. They come here with high expectations, and then when the bubble bursts, the disappointment is so big that it turns to chaos. *The way you lead says a lot about you.* Do you have dignity? Past leaders knew who they were and what they were fighting for. *I am more unsympathetic now* with students and with their cause because they don't seem to know what their cause is.

Jolene points to the Steve Biko Building where student leadership meetings usually take place.

> **Jolene:** Yes, nowadays it seems that students don't have reasoning skills. Just shouting. Entitlement. I just feel that when we were students the leadership had more structure; there were rules of engagement. But the current group… *I don't know what the focus is.* Even back when I was in student leadership, *I didn't have a voice. I was a messenger.* The other 'radical' leaders bulldozed us. Told us what they wanted. Our voices were not heard. As coloured leaders,[1] our voices were not heard. We are not black and we are not white, so we fall between the cracks. They said, 'Jansen must go!'[2] And we didn't have a voice. I remember the night

after Shimla Park. We could not leave campus. There were messages on WhatsApp. Threats from right-wing white groups. We were going to protect the residence. Five girls – black and white – were ready to protect our residence. It was scary; something else. We were students and we did not know what to do, but we could see that the residence head also didn't know what to do.

Riley circles a different site on the same map.

Riley: The symbols and the statues. So, eventually, with this uproar last year, I challenged the guys and told them we have to start rethinking. One night, I got a tip-off that some guys were coming. Told the guys we are removing the things to another location. Got recommendations that we really should revisit our symbols; remove things that are not representative of who we are these days as a university. Now we have photos of the rector in the hall. To change traditions was difficult. I had to get into their heads. Senior guys became my friends. I learned that the oldest man is the highest authority and to get their trust and support, I had to get the oldest man on my side; I will have his back. Because I knew he was very influential. The next Prime (residence student leader) said, *change is gonna happen and prepare yourself for that*. It was a white boy who said that. Now we are in a space where the residence is transformed in terms of culture and symbols. *So decolonization; yes, the past is gone now*. We have our own new identity. But many white boys moved out of res. The guys are not comfortable with change and where we are going. It is unfortunate that the way we are raised indoctrinates us. We come to a space where we are supposed to think critically and we still have a boxed view. So, I told them when you go into the workforce one day, you will be stretched. I left them with that. Some thought about it, others just didn't care. Nowadays they go off campus. For me that's sad because they can still add value to the space.

    I wasn't here when Shimla Park happened. I came here just after all that happened. When I became a residence head, I was stuck in between two groups of students. Last year, I was stretched tremendously. I was called a racist and names. The black students said I was siding with the white students. I was actually sick and had to be booked off on leave for two months. We wanted to get everyone on equal footing. Both sides were making the space uncomfortable for everybody. It was a real challenge. *I learned to listen more*. The guys wanted to change traditions and I told them *how* you want to do it is important. Some guys just wanted to be too radical. Most white boys moved out of the residence because of the change. I came in just after the protest and I had to keep both sides happy. It was a challenge. This whole change and transformation thing has a three-year process. We now came to a point where no funny stuff is happening. *That transformation had taught me a lot about myself* and how to be a better leader.

Anne shifts uncomfortably in her chair. She doesn't touch the map.

> **Anne:** I don't know. I don't know what to say. I am an overthinker, I find it very difficult. I am struggling with the language thing. The whole thing about Afrikaans; I am Afrikaans. Where does Afrikaans fit in when we move to a more afro-centric/African identity? *I don't think I have a lot of influence.*

> **Book:** Marguerite is trying to write this chapter. But her attention is elsewhere. Her mind keeps drifting away from the page in front of her and she finds herself staring out of the window. The campus is like a ghost town. There is no one walking about, no one laughing, no human in sight. Just birds. Ever since the national lockdown, the sounds of the birds have replaced the usual human noises. Everyone is working from home, and in her case, campus is home. She feels lonely and it is difficult to connect to the work in front of her. Everything she does seems trivial in the face of what is happening around them. In a matter of a few weeks, the entire world has changed. Everything has ground to a sudden halt. The COVID-19 pandemic has changed the lives and thoughts of people across the globe. Then, there is the constant stream of WhatsApp messages from family, friends and students. When she is not checking WhatsApp, she turns to the latest news pages: How many deaths? How many infections? Where is the epicentre of this disease now? And who is next? Through the distractions, she tries to read an article Liezl had sent her. She prints out the article, gets up from her laptop, leaves her phone on the desk and walks outside. There is a sunny spot on her children's trampoline and she takes her reading there. Away from her phone and her laptop, it becomes easier to focus. The printed pages in her hand move lightly in the breeze; the autumn sun warms her feet and the trampoline rocks gently beneath her and calms her anxious thoughts. Looking forward is looking back; she remembers from the last chapter ... but where did all this start?
>
> When we write the story of ourselves and the story of others, these stories often intertwine in such a way that the one cannot really exist without the

others. But also, when we write a story, there is often the desire to give it a beginning, a middle and an end; however, when we look at subjectivity as an assembled multiplicity, the stories we tell cannot really function in a linear timeline. For example, in the article Marguerite is reading, Maria Tamboukou (2010) traces women artists' nomadic paths of resisting what they are and becoming other (p. 681). She describes her project as being in the fold between life and art. The stories we tell are, similarly, in the fold between education/art and life. Tamboukou challenges an 'image of narratives as unified and coherent representations of lives and subjects' and, instead, turns our attention to their ability to open up 'microsociological analyses of deterritorializations and lines of flight' (2010, 681). So, when we create our cartographies of becoming educators, we are not really trying to make sense of everything that has happened to us. We are trying to discover what all of this is asking of us. We are looking at how we have been shaped by the events and experiences and objects in this space. Tamboukou (2010, 683) considers education to be a site where juxtaposing discourses can show how the private and public lives of women can show resistance and becoming other. In our narrative, we offer a similar juxtaposition of the private and public lives of students who became educators and educators were once students. These lives are situated in a time of rapid social change and protest in a particular context.

But where did all this start? I am a book and they are writing me. So, when exactly did I come into being? Was it when Marguerite and Liezl sat down to write a book proposal? Was it when they did their PhDs? Was it the first time they met, many years ago, when they were just kids? Was it when they were born? Or when they came to work at the UFS? Was it the night of Shimla Park? Or was I here all along, a virtual potentiality of becoming *book*?

6.2.3 A Story without a Beginning or an Ending

This is not a linear story. It is a story without a beginning or an end. The different lines of our narratives tread through the present, the past and a potential future. Cartography makes it possible for the story to emerge in nested time and memory (Koro-Ljungberg and Hendricks 2018). Koro-Ljungberg and Hendricks draw on Bergson and Deleuze to 'rethink time as a mass of connecting differences' (2018, 1). The implication is that the past exists in the present and 'time can never be disconnected from that which precedes it' (Koro-Ljungberg and Hendricks 2018, 4). Time being multiple implies that it does not only belong to individuals who contract life in the present (active syntheses) but also involves the pre-personal 'process of the individuation and change' (Koro-Ljungberg and Hendricks 2018, 5) (passive synthesis). The concept of nested time helps us to think differently about lives, narratives and memories as we move away from an essentialized and psychologized understanding of identity towards a subjectivity that is assembled as the various flows of life are contracted by a subject in the present (Müller, Kruger and Le Roux, 2021).

Perhaps, the question Marguerite should be asking is not, *where* did all this start? Or, *when* did all this start? but rather, *what* does this make possible?

6.2.4 What Does This Make Possible?

The story we tell is like a nest or a web, or a rhizome, where the different lines meet and diverge and come together again to form a non-linear narrative of becoming educators. We, the humans in this narrative, come together in a certain moment of time, because of the work we do and the place where we work. There are Marguerite and Liezl, asking the questions and writing the book. Then there is Riley who wants his story to inspire students; Annie who wanted to be a pilot but was rejected and has learned from that rejection; Elize who wants to be part of something bigger than herself; Lizzy whose patience is wearing thin; Jolene who feels unsympathetic; and Dan who is here and not in prison, not in parliament and not dead. And then, of course, there is the place, the space and the more-than-human parts of this story that all entangle in what we call Book. In Chapter 7 we will offer an exploration of the more-than-human elements of this narrative.

We meet in a room with a heavy wooden table and a big window where afternoon sunlight filters in through the blinds. There are black-and-white lino-cut artworks on the off-white walls. On the table are some snacks, drawing material and a recording device. We are colleagues and we chat informally for a while before Liezl switches on the recording device.

> **Marguerite:** Please use the paper and drawing materials provided and draw your journey. How did you get here, to where you are now?

Riley draws a cricket bat and colours it green. He draws a hockey stick and a rugby ball.

> When I grew up I played a lot of sport, I played hockey, rugby.

He draws a building and writes UFS under it. He colours it orange. He draws a red arrow pointing downwards and writes 'FAIL' on it.

> I wanted to study in Cape Town but was convinced to study in Bloem. I became distracted by a girl. I felt vulnerable. I failed.

He draws himself in conversation with a mentor. He draws a green arrow pointing upwards and writes 'PASS' on it.

> I got a *second chance* to study. There was a prof who spoke to me. Like a father to a son. I will always be grateful to him. He gave me the realities of life. It was an aha moment – someone is seeing my potential that I can't see myself. It was a *turning point* in my life. He believed in me and I produced the results.

He draws himself in front of the class.

> I made *a success* of it, and now I want to be a positive influence on others. I like teaching and engaging with students. I want to be *a positive influence* on them. I can relate to what students go through. I want my story *to inspire*. I want my story *to influence* others.

> **Book:** When did Riley become an educator – the day he failed or the day he passed?

> **Liezl:** Please tell us about your journey. How did you get here – to where you are now?

Annie gets emotional when she talks about her life story.

> Sorry, guys, I don't know what's up.

She draws an army tank and colours it green. She draws a butterfly and a rainbow – her grandparents, a little girl in a pink dress with a dog and a bicycle. A smiling sun and flowers.

> I had a happy childhood. I grew up on a military base. I grew up pretty privileged. I remember nature and the mountains of Lesotho. *Life was good.*

She draws a church. She draws an academic achievement award. She colours both orange.

> The *church* played a big role. At school I was considered an *academic giant*. I got awards. I became the *first black head girl* of a mostly white school. *Or coloured or whatever* you want to call it. I think I have issues with identity and all *these categories*!

She draws a helicopter and colours it blue.

> I always wanted to join the air force. But it never really worked out for me, kind of *a rejection*.

Annie's voice becomes full and tearful as she talks of the rejection she felt. She draws a pair of glasses.

> Varsity opened my eyes. I grew up with a safety net, sheltered. I was sent to a 'Christian National' school. At varsity I *became really free to question* things and be myself. *Here I am now*.
>
> **Book:** When did Annie become an educator? *After* she was rejected'? When did she become free to question?

> **Marguerite:** Talk to us about your drawing, how did you get to where you are now?

Elize draws a little hut.

> **Elize**: I was born to a European mom and African dad. I was brought up on the farm. *I struggled with identity* because I was the light little one. I suffered from neglect from my mom's side because she also struggled with my identity. I went to a Model C,³ 'British English' school. Developed myself as an individual, got involved with *politics*. Prof. Jansen came to my school and said 'oh, a *black head girl*'; he invited me to UFS. I got involved in politics, sometimes your *liberal ways*, fighting for *the good*, are not accepted amongst others. I am very *feminist*. Very for the *community*. Now I find myself in research. Humanitarian changes. *I want to be part of something bigger than myself*.

Dan points to his drawing of a graveyard and a prison cell.

> **Dan**: Well here I am; I am not in prison, I am not in parliament, I am not dead.
>
> **Book:** How did Dan, Elize, Annie and Riley become educators?

6.2.5 Becoming Educators

By thinking about educator subjectivity, we are interested in how educator subjectivity is shaped during a time of rapid social change. The subjectifying moment is, according to Biesta, the moment when the subject meets the choice, 'meet the possibility of doing a or b, that suddenly sort of pulls you into the world' (2020, 103).

> That is, in my view, a very relational moment because *you encounter 'something' that comes to you* and were it is then up to you and no one else to figure out what to do … This [choice] is not about ethical categories; it's not about good or bad or about an obligation to do good. It is also not a rational choice. But it is about meeting a choice – which also means meeting your own freedom – and in that moment meeting yourself, so to speak. So for me it's actually that you could say that the choice produces the subject. Or maybe it is better to say the choice is subjectifying because it bring you into play. (Biesta 2020a, 103–4)

In our cartography of different narratives, we see the way a certain event or moment brings educator subjectivity into play. The lives of the people who participated in our research are intertwined with the subjectifying moments that they choose to accept, or receive as a 'gift'. At the heart of subjectification is the 'whole challenge of existing in the world but not as object, but as subject' (Biesta 2020a, 110). Our narrative shows how educators become subjects by existing in the world. During the COVID-19 pandemic, we are living, once again, through another

> critical moment – a time of 'crisis', which should not be understood as chaos, but, going back to the Greek word 'krinein', as a turning point that calls for judgment. Less than the modern optimism of 'What shall we do?' or, in more shallow form, 'What do we fancy?', we are faced with a different question: 'What is this asking from us?' (Biesta 2020b, 30)

If we think of teaching as a way to help our students to '*pay attention, individually and collectively*' (Biesta 2020b, 31), then we also need to pay attention to the moments and events when/where educators become subjects, individually and collectively. In other words, our cartography is an attempt to pay attention to the events or moments when educator subjectivity emerges during a time of crisis or rapid change.

6.2.6 Paying Attention to the Event

Something happened… it was like a spark that ignited a fire… but the potential of the fire was there before the spark and the glowing embers remained long after – ready to spark again.

There was the night of Shimla Park. There was everything that came before it. The weeks that followed and the years that rolled by. In this book, the narratives of becoming educators criss-cross and meet at this 'wound-event'.

Jolene: We went to the rugby field, we were waiting for the match to start and we saw a group of students moving onto the field. *Chaos erupted.* We took the first-year students back to the residence and had a meeting with the residence head. From that specific day it was *constant meetings* on campus. We met at Steve Biko House on campus. Lots of meetings. There were threats on WhatsApp, racial attacks from white to black and black to white. Girls moved out of residences. *As leaders, we were anxious, but we were ready to stand in front of the door*, black and white together. Some leaders resigned. It was traumatic. 2016!

Lizzy: But there is always polarization; I always feel polarized. I try to make it into something positive. Small things, like arriving at the meeting without an agenda, makes you feel marginalized. There's a lot of it in life, but just get over it. I have always tried to connect people through sport. I was also in leadership in 2016. *After the Shimla incident, it was like watching the people you were leading with changing into people you don't know*. It was scary and I was alone. I did not know what was happening. That first night was rough – I heard petrol bombs. And then waking up and not having class. I remember the desolation of campus at the end of 2016. Never knowing who you're gonna meet around the next corner. I had to take my guide dog off campus, because I felt he might even antagonize people more. Fragile dog. I feared for the dog. Very dark time in our history. That desolate kind of feeling on campus. *How people changed*. Wondering if they felt like this all the time. I felt betrayed. Like I could not trust anyone. I felt betrayed.

Elize: During Shimla Park I was very involved as a student leader. I lived close to the main gate. Lots of things happened – a nationwide protest and we were trying to stand together as students, *but management didn't understand. We were together for the future good for students with similar backgrounds like us*. It got crazy at a certain point. It was the first week after Shimla Park. The police came. I was in my room, and could hear the commotion in the corridors, and then I just saw a gun opening my window. I was sitting at my desk at the window, and he is opening my window with a gun. I am screaming and running out of my room, 'have I seen right?' Then he threw a gas thing in my room. They are there with a list and saying we are hiding people. Where are we hiding these people, I ask?

Dan: There was an altercation with the white girl where a megaphone and a black guy with dreadlocks were involved. People were looking for someone with dreadlocks, so people cut their dreadlocks the same day.

So they were not suspects anymore because they didn't have dreadlocks. Quite fascinating.

Elize: Sometimes, when white people see a black person's picture, they think it looks like any black person. Black person. Dreadlocks. Not realistic to break into another person's home. *You just don't do it.* They are sorry afterwards about the gas in my room.

Dan: So, I was never there when the cops were breaking into things. I walked past Madelief. I saw people running and the police were looking for people with political regalia. But then the students had to leave and I went into the quad, chilled. I was getting feed from people, sending me pictures and information and the teargas. But then people broke into my own place, *so I couldn't go back.*

Marguerite: I was walking outside with the baby and I saw the police vehicles coming and the students running. I was shocked. To see the violence the students were arrested with. I had the baby and I had to get inside and spoke to the residence committee and told them they must close the doors. My husband came home, but I told him he shouldn't come out. It became very personal for us who lived on campus. I was worried about our safety. But the students were scared too. Everyone was scared. 'Don't worry Ma'am we will protect you and your baby', one student sent me a message. But it was my job to protect them. *I felt very confused.* Campus gates got closed; Liezl couldn't come out and I had to take her food – I just remember taking a broccoli! That is all I remember. My son asked me, 'Who are these guys sitting at the gate?' Riot police: it was strange explaining that to my child.

Liezl: Mpho called me. I was naïve because I have never been in a protest. I went out and the protesters confronted me. I realized too late there is nothing I could do. I thought I was going out to show my solidarity as a white person, but it backfired. So, Tsepho came and diffused the situation. *It was a crucial moment, realizing the extent of the racial division.* After Shimla Park, things are much more complicated for me. It opened my eyes and race things are much more complicated. Everything is kind of grey. So, in the messages from management there was this clear distinction between protesters and students, but actually they were the same.

Elize: That same night a white Afrikaner group posted on WhatsApp. They said 'we will not allow these kids to disrupt our education; we are gonna beat them up'. Two days before that, we were arrested at the gate and there was a big bang and we all started running. A policeman grabbed me, I spat at him after he swore at me with a racial term. *And I was arrested*. I really felt as leaders we were not being heard. We supported the protesting students with food and water. Instead, we were treated like we are against the university. We fought for the cause, but we also wanted to show the university that you can do this without being so violent. There was a special hotel for people who felt unsafe and the white kids went there – they were allowed to say they were scared. *I, as a black kid, was not allowed to say I feel unsafe*. And why I feel ostracized now is *because of what happened after Shimla Park*.

6.2.7 To Disrupt and Encounter

In the previous section, we paid attention to the 'event' as a meeting point between the different stories and narratives in this chapter. The event is something that draws coherence to the narrative and, at the same time, disrupts. By foregrounding a critical event, we are able to focus on the backgrounds of the narrative. The event is thus a node or knot where the narratives intersect or criss-cross. However, the event is surrounded by, informed by and infused by the event, the everyday, ordinary moments that might remain unexplored in the background.

This process of narrative cohesion around a significant event organizes and realigns experiences to achieve unity. The events of the narrative experience draw attention from those particular everyday qualities of experience, leaving them already in place. But what of the everyday experiences (Boulton-Funke 2014, 6)?

In thinking about educator subjectivity, we need to shift our attention from the 'critical moments' in the narrative to the everyday experiences and backgrounds that disrupt rather than affirm our understandings (Boulton-Funke 2014). This is where cartography is a useful tool because it gives us a way to conflate all memory, experience, events, places, objects and affects that emerge from the narratives. This might be a way to move beyond the tracing of identity formation as linear and progressive, to something more complex and dynamic.

Arts-based research helps us link the past and the present 'prosthetically' (Finley 2017, 565). However, arts-based research also helps us to disrupt and 'to tear down and reconfigure the traditional dichotomies of art/science, nature/culture, natural/artificial, incorporeality/materiality, subjectivity/objectivity, sense/effect, or body/thought' (Finley 2017, 563). Finley refers to the political power of resistance that resides in critical arts-based inquiry where 'researchers perform inquiry that is cutting edge and seeks to perform and inspire socially just, emancipatory, and transformative political acts' (2017, 252). Critical arts-based research is aimed at creating work that can disrupt the status quo and reveal power imbalances instead of reducing itself to a representation of power (Finley 2017, 569).

Our aim was to work beyond a representation of the experiences or lives of the becoming educators in order to gain a new understanding of educator subjectivities. We used cartography as a tool for arts-based inquiry. Ulmer and Koro-Ljungberg 'conceptualize cartography not as a prescriptive navigational formula, but as a fluid, dynamic process for exploration and experimentation in research and writing – as experimentation that works against linguistic fascism and cultural grand narratives' (2015, 139). Our use of cartography is centred around the use of a campus map, but the map is a mere entry point into a more complex, non-linear, unfolding narrative. Our intention is, thus, not to trace, but to map. 'Deleuze and Guattari (2008) suggest that the act of interpreting experience requires a tracing of connections and that a more generative process is developed through the concept of mapping. In this process connections are made forming new assemblages' (Boulton-Funke 2014, 9). Ulmer and Koro-Ljungberg (2015, 139) explain Deleuze and Guattari's differentiation between tracing and mapping by looking at sedentary cartography, or tracing as something that remains fixed in place, whereas nomadic cartography, or maps, travel through space. The move, from tracing experience to mapping encounters, might generate new possibilities; it can be seen as a 'shift from representing to doing, [because] contemporary art practice and research become invested in the provocation of thought that disrupts habits of mind and performance of habit' (Boulton-Funke 2014, 13).

Therefore, we wanted to map, not trace, how educator subjectivity forms and evolves as it travels through space – not to interpret the process but rather to form new assemblages of becoming educators. We generated a narrative through our mapping of the drawings, recordings, memories, objects and other elements of the research process. Our writing process drew on visual elements and started with a shape rather than a text or an image; in other words, 'a linguistically empty canvas' (Ulmer and Koro-Ljungberg 2015, 146). Writing visually becomes a way for Ulmer and Koro-Ljungberg to engage with blank cartography:

> Not yet written cartography, therefore, becomes the blank canvass for analyzing and conceptualizing emergent pathways. Writing and research events in this article grow from blank cartography, a linguistically empty canvas (only shapes,

no text or images), and hanging extensions of unresolved analysis. Cartography becomes a complementary means of conceptualizing career pathways across education (Ulmer and Koro-Ljungberg 2015, 144).

In this cartography of educator becomings, we think of research 'as an invitation to re-encounter' (Boulton-Funke 2014, 12). As we did this, we were conscious of the critical moment or event, making it possible to talk about change and transformation in our space, 'yet in the narrative form the daily practices are left in-place and normalized rendering the subject produced by that which is already in place leaving those normative practices un-scrutinized' (Boulton-Funke 2014, 6). Thus, we would like to move beyond thinking about the narrative event to the encounter because '[t]he encounter creates resistance or disruption to normative thought by drawing on the affective disruption to perceptions' (Boulton-Funke 2014, 8).

The encounter denies this process of interpretation and representation by disrupting that which is already in place and, in doing so, new potentials for practices and place become possible. The encounter shifts attention to the tacit or silent by disrupting the continuity and unification of the narrative event and, in doing so, inquiry shifts, from narrative as representing, to narrative as provoking. The conception of identity becomes a dynamic and continuous reflexive account of processes of becoming where the self is conceptualized as entangled, contingent, non-uniform and incomplete, emerging and re-emerging (Boulton-Funke 2014, 7).

In this story, we hoped that cartography could help us think beyond the narrative events in becoming-educator narratives to engage with the encounters. In this way, we hoped we could think of subjectivity and becoming-educators as messy, non-linear unfoldings that do not follow any logical progression. We wanted to show how the event and the disruption in the narrative becomes a point where becoming emerges; and also a point to which it returns and re-emerges. The event might shape us and call us back, time and again, and in each encounter, we need to pay attention to what is being asked of us.

6.2.8 A Story without an Ending

Marguerite: How have you changed?
Jolene: I have learned I must be careful what you say and how you say it to students in current space. Careful and cautious.

Elize: The people that are in management remember everything; you don't forget people who are outspoken about injustices. That played a part in my identity on campus. Now I am not really included in what is happening on campus. I stay away from these things. I think people will say 'Elize, she is too outspoken. She is an angry black woman', without knowing what we went through as student leaders.

Dan: Ever since my department found out I was part of the #FeesMustFall movement, the treatment changed. But I think these were the ramifications of being so involved.

Marguerite: You speak a lot about the negative consequences. What would be positive?

Riley: I got a call from Columbia University the other day. A student saying thank you. It makes it all worthwhile.

Dan: You get to know your limits, you become more conscious of how society function. I wouldn't call it benefits. Some students, they praised us, they would see you as a revolutionary, and you would become popular. You become well known if you are a mouthpiece for a student movement.

Elize: I am multiracial, whatever; mixed race. I became so racist, and my mom said, 'no, no, you can't be like this'. And all of this Shimla Park took me back again. Campus was a space where I could not be myself. I was angered when I saw what the others went through. I was accepted as an older leader and respected, but I won't call it a good thing. It's not something I would write on my CV. I would not be involved in the protest now, I will just look at the dynamics of protest. Take the recent gender protest; the dynamic is so different than the way we would protest. A bit ill-informed, too emotional and not coming from sense; it's just a thing of, we have to protest. People started to stampede. I don't think protests are well thought through any longer on campus. Now, protesting is not only for the right reasons. I don't give my two cents in front of masses.

Liezl: You talk about your involvement in protest and how it has changed. What has changed now that you have shifted from student to staff member?

Dan: Now it would be conflict of interest… so, now we sometimes have mini protests. If I am teaching and the protesters come. I can just conclude the lesson. I just go out and say, 'hey, Thabo, I am almost done there'. So I use my privilege to negotiate with protesters. I haven't changed. I was always very composed in this difficult situations. I never run. I go and talk to cops. The change is always gonna be on a personal level. You reflect more. And you become more conscious.

Elize: I make life very easy for my students, put things online and [give] extensions for tests. Department felt I was spoon-feeding them. I continue with political conversation; students must know their rights and have to question their governance. I succeeded in that; some of them are in public forums and working in the glass house… To be honest, I shut the protest out of my conscious mind. What I got out of the protest? To speak for myself and to fight for myself. We were in jail together – all of us boys and girls in the cell and it was fun. It was a moment in my life – powerful. I can now speak up for others and for myself. It changed my opinion of how management and governance work within higher education. How management see us just as a number. Management took themselves out of the campus. Made us look like walking criminals rather than people that management should be looking out for.

Marguerite: So, in terms of the call for decolonization, transformation, where are we now?

Elize: A lot of white people left campus and varsity after Shimla Park, and those who stayed just come to class. So this created a more black campus in terms of participation. Has this moved us towards integrating? No, it hasn't. But you can't force white people to integrate. But does it create a space where black people can interact with whites? No. There are still racial dynamics on campus.

Dan: Transformation, decolonization – it's mostly quite pretentious rhetoric. The progress we made is mostly on paper. My examiner didn't want to pass me because I didn't have an Afrikaans summary. He was an external examiner. If he insists on this. I refused; I was passive aggressive. Things have to change outside for things to change inside. We come from outside and then come inside. If things are not changing outside, it won't change inside. I understand why people think it should be in reverse, the university being a microcosm. But if the inequality outside doesn't change, the inside won't change. The bigger structurers must change. *A university is a drop in the ocean.*

Elize: If students don't see people like them educating them, this is as far as they think they can go. We need more people of colour in academia and in the rectorate.

Dan: Quite simple. I think about my potential, jack of all trades. I am trying to find a focus. Social science, sport science, journalism, interest in academia, but from which angle. Also won't mind being in entertainment. Even if it's just one that I am very good at. It's a constant struggle.

Elize: Society wants us to get married and have kids, but it's not my plan. I would like to create social justice and social cohesion. Meaningful resolution. Higher education capabilities. Classism. Take away this obstacle – class should not define you.

Lizzy: We are in a powerful position to influence. We must never forget it and we must live our lives accordingly. If you don't want to do that, you should not be in this space. The most important thing I had to learn was to set boundaries and they hated me for it. It was difficult. The students hated me for it. They saw it as unavailability. *I had to learn to say, Can you please come back later?*

6.2.9 New Possibilities

Things come and go, even if they are cast in bronze.
Marguerite plays hide and seek with her children in the Red Square.
Her daughter likes to hide in the shadow of the massive base of the big Steyn statue.
One day, there is a big crane and the statue is hoisted up into the blue Bloemfontein sky.[4]
Now the hiding place is gone.
But there is more space to roller skate and ride a bike.
With the stature gone there is more space to play.

6.3 What the Cartography Makes Possible

In this chapter, we used cartography as a tool for doing research as well as for interpreting research. It helped us make sense of the non-linear formation and becoming of assembled educator subjectivities in a space where rapid social changes are taking place. Here, subjectivity merges with place and space through encounters, events, disruptions and interruptions to formulate new possibilities.

Our cartography functions within narrative and arts-based traditions of inquiry. We were interested in how the narratives of different participants who were student leaders and who then became educators during a volatile time of change and student protest at the UFS in South Africa. The flow between student and staff experiences made interesting connections possible for viewing the formulation of educator subjectivity as something messy, incoherent and ruptured. In this sense, cartography made it possible to look at subjectivity as an assemblage rather than a coherent and logical development. Loots et al. (2017, 108) write about a Western narrative tradition in which the coherent subject is one in which we can makes sense of past, present and future experiences as part of a meaningful whole. However, cartography makes it possible to see multiple entry points that open up a space where the subject is no longer coherent, whole and closed, but rather 'diverse, fragmented, contradictory and open' (Loots et al. 2017, 109). Through cartography, we offer different points of entry into lives, experiences, memories and performances of becoming-educator subjectivity:

> There is no right entryway that will lead the researcher to the truth/the reality about an individual. The illusion that there is such a thing as one entryway that leads to the real self is completely given up. The rhizomatic self has many possible entryways and every entry will lead to other connections, and different versions of selfhood in which the one is not more 'true' than the other. Which entryway is taken and which connections there are made during the speaking, depends on the context in which the telling takes place. This is so because, in the telling, there is always the other. (Loots et al. 2017, 111)

Thus, it becomes possible to think of becoming-educator subjectivity as the ability to shape and reshape continuously. Freed from the desire to see subjects as stable or orderly, we can make unexpected connections with place, space, other and self. In our narrative, becoming an educator means finding new entryways into the world, and in each encounter, we ask, what does this make possible?

6.4 Some Ideas for Using Cartography

In writing this chapter, we used cartography as a tool to explore educator subjectivity and becoming during a time of rapid social change at the UFS. Through drawing and mapping, we were able to think of our performed or narrated selves as a line that criss-crosses other lines in a non-linear story of becoming educators. However, the line is always drawn on a surface, or the reserve: 'the concept of the surface as a reserve ensures that no drawing is ever finished. The last line to have been drawn is never the last that could have been drawn' (Ingold 2010, 301). In the next chapter (Chapter 7), we will explore the reserve, or surface, of the line. In this chapter, we used cartography to help us draw lines that show 'a history of becoming, rather than an image of being' (Ingold 2010, 301). Below, we unpack some of the specific steps we took and questions we asked as we explored the multiple entryways into a narrative of students who became educators in this space. We hope that this could serve as a starting point for those who wish to embark on research into educator identity using cartography.

1. *Start by looking at a blank, or surface*

    - What does a blank page make possible?
    - What does it ask of us?

2. *Make a line drawing of your journey of becoming*

    - Where are you now?
    - How did you get here?
    - What did you encounter along the way?
    - What did these encounters ask of you?
    - How are you different now?
    - Where does your line criss-cross the lines of others?

3. *Use a map of the space in which we find ourselves*

    - Show the places/spaces where you have had significant encounters.
    - What did these encounters ask from you?

7

More than Human: An Exploration of the Entanglement of Educator Subjectivity and Space

Space [is] the dimension of multiple trajectories, a simultaneity of stories-so-far. Space [is] the dimension of a multiplicity of durations.
– (Massey 2005, 24)

The material form of a pencil is shaped by the anticipation of the future possibility of writing with it.
– (Rosiek and Snyder 2018, 5)

7.1 Interviewing the More than Human

We wrote this chapter in collaboration with Frans Kruger, who has worked with walking as post-humanist transformative pedagogy (Kruger 2020). Kruger helps us to think of place as more than a backdrop to a narrative by making the argument that place 'is not an ontological "thing" or essence, but and unfolding event' (2020, 328). The place we explore is the UFS campus. If we consider this specific place as 'emergent, agentic and relational' (Kruger 2020, 329), it allows us to be attentive to subjectivity as an entangled expression of human and more-than-human. We understand space and place to express different ideas. Space is more general and abstract, while place is more specific. At the same time, our use of the term space as general should be understood to incorporate place as specific.

In this chapter, we will look at post-humanist understandings of subjectivity to view it as an assemblage of aesthetic encounters that creates new possibilities of being. The crisis of representation, and by extension, reterritorialization, has highlighted the problematic nature of humanist notions of subjectivity that plague research methodologies, including arts-based inquiry (Boulton-Funke 2014, 106). For Boulton-Funke (2014), a post-qualitative approach to arts-based and narrative research challenges the coherent, linear, stable subject, by turning our attention to the mundane event. In this chapter, we will take up such a challenge by asking what inquiry does instead of asking what it means.

We combined arts-based inquiry with walking as a method of inquiry to explore the assemblage of becoming-educators at the UFS. We view space and the more-than-human as a research participant, while also seeing ourselves as respondents to space, and the encounters we might have during our walking. A notion of 'space as open, multiple and relational, unfinished and always becoming' (Massey 2005, 58) is integral to our inquiry into and encounter with multiple trajectories and narratives during our walking:

> In spatial configurations, otherwise unconnected narratives may be brought into contact, or previously connected ones may be wrenched apart. There is always an element of 'chaos'. *This is the chance of space*; the accidental neighbour is one figure for it. Space as the closed system of the essential section presupposes (guarantees) the singular universal. But in this other spatiality different temporalities and different voices must work out means of accommodation. *The chance of space must be responded to.* (Massey 2005, 111; emphasis added)

Space is multiplicity and the meeting of trajectories, stories and histories. Our inquiry/walking follows this negotiation with multiple human/non-human trajectories and narratives. During our inquiry, we created the space relationally with humans and the more-than-human, and you will meet them shortly: the earth, trees, water, birds, fences, buildings, statues, artworks. The sounds of birds, and their behaviour, formed refrains that territorialized the space – we were thrown together in this space, and we had to enter into negotiations with these refrains involuntarily – which reminded us that the more-than-human can also demand negotiations, have expressive qualities and can participate in practices of art-making:

> Art is not the privilege of human beings. Messiaen is right in saying that many birds are not only virtuosos but artists, above all in their territorial songs … The refrain is rhythm and melody that have been territorialized because they have become expressive – and have become expressive because they are territorializing. We are not going in circles. What we wish to say is that there is a self-movement of expressive qualities. (Deleuze and Guattari 2008, 316–17)

Space is relational and subjectivities are constituted in and with space. It is exactly because of the relational dimension of subjectivity that terms of engagement of relations should hence be interrogated (Massey 2005, 180). 'Place … change[s] us … through the practising of space, the negotiation of intersecting trajectories; place [is] an arena where negotiation is forced upon us' (Massey 2005, 154). Space is negotiated, multiple, always under construction, open and never finished. We create space; it is not given nor static. The event of place, where multiple trajectories (stories, narratives) meet, involves a process of negotiation (Massey 2005).

We 'interviewed' the narrative space by walking through it. Kruger explores 'the way in which knowledge grows as one walks through/in place' (2020, 330). He goes on to argue that, through walking, we can transform the world because it is 'a means of border crossing, observation, asking, listening and conversing' (Kruger 2020, 331) that allows learning to take place. This notion enables us to think of 'walking as a method of cartography that maps relations of power but at the same time also interrogates these relations in order to experiment with the creation of different knowledges' (Kruger 2020, 331). 'The fact that knowledge grows as we move through place foregrounds that it emerges with/in a specific place and time for a specific purpose, the implications of which is that knowledge-growing is a political and ethical activity' (Kruger 2020, 335).

We walked through the space. We also walked through the narratives that had emerged in this space. We were walking through the past, the present and the future. We moved along the line drawn by the narratives in Chapter 6. The line always exists in a reserve and the reserve contains the potential, or virtuality, of that which has not yet been drawn.

Ingold is inspired by the work of Norman Bryson and thinks of drawing as a reserve, which relieves the line of the responsibility to always put the totality first: 'the concept of the surface as a reserve ensures that no drawing is ever finished. The last line to have been drawn is never the last that could have been drawn' (Ingold 2010, 301). Lines and narratives have this in common: 'In life as in drawing, what is done cannot be undone. You can only carry on from where you are now, leaving a trail behind you as evidence of where you have been' (Ingold 2010, 304). Our walking thus followed lines that cannot be undone because the stories have been told. The narratives that shaped the line we walked were active agents in the research process; in other words, we worked with 'the idea that the stories we tell are themselves agents' (Rosiek and Snyder 2018, 9). As we walked through the space, we tried to practice research that does not consume or produce but rather responds to what is already there.

7.2 Walking the Line

What if the living being is the line of its own movement?

(Ingold 2010, 300).

In Chapter 6, we show how the cartographies of becoming-educators at the UFS helped us to draw lines on a surface. The lines that we trace in this chapter are based on the stories of important places and affective incidents as they relate to instances of social transformation at the UFS, and the way these were experienced by various educators. In working with subjectivity, we need to make it clear that we understand it, not as a given, but as something that must be worked at continuously. We are thus involved with the world in a never-ending process of remaking ourselves. Subjectification stands central to this process and unfolds with the 'movement of the world's self-surpassing' (Ingold 2010, 304). It is this process of becoming that allows for the foregrounding of the importance of creativity and improvisation. The narratives the educators shared prompted us to 'follow the materials, to copy the gestures, and to draw the lines' (Ingold 2010, 304). Rosiek and Snyder (2018, 2) argue that, from a new materialist position, stories that emerge in narrative forms of research are agents themselves and not merely representational. For them, 'narratives become descriptions of particular complex possibilities for future being that exist whether or not they are actualized. Their possibility influences the present – gives the present its form' (Rosiek and Snyder 2018, 9). The narratives that emerged from and within the space were used to draw a virtual line through the space. We focused on places that the educators we interviewed had cited as significant or affective. Narratives have agency and hence determined our route and guided the line. We then used the physical action of walking on the virtual line through the space and engaged with the space as research participants. By walking, we both followed the materials/narratives, and drew on the reserve. We were, thus, engaging with the narratives as more than human 'agents' who are shaped by the anticipation of the future possibility. As Rosiek and Snyder explain, 'The material form of a pencil is shaped by the anticipation of the future possibility of writing with it' (2018, 5).

Thus, drawing carries on to form a history of becoming, rather than an image of being. Our tracing of a line on a surface or in a space was thus not aimed at creating a complete picture, but rather at drawing attention to the togethering of persons and things in a specific time and place. We thought of place as a research participant in our pursuit to explore educator subjectivity during a time of transformation and change.

We do not aim to present a complete description of what was there or what we experienced, but rather to show the joining together with persons and other things in the movement of their formation. What we did, then, was 'a participatory act of togethering' (Ingold 2010, 304) with the world with which we moved as we drew a line. The line was also what guided us – thus, not a pre-determined 'method' that shaped our thinking but rather a guide to which we affectively responded to in a post-qualitative (St. Pierre 2019) approach to inquiry. The line we walked is thus envisioned as a non-human participant in our injury. It is a shape that gives our actions and thoughts shape. We created the line, but the line also creates us.

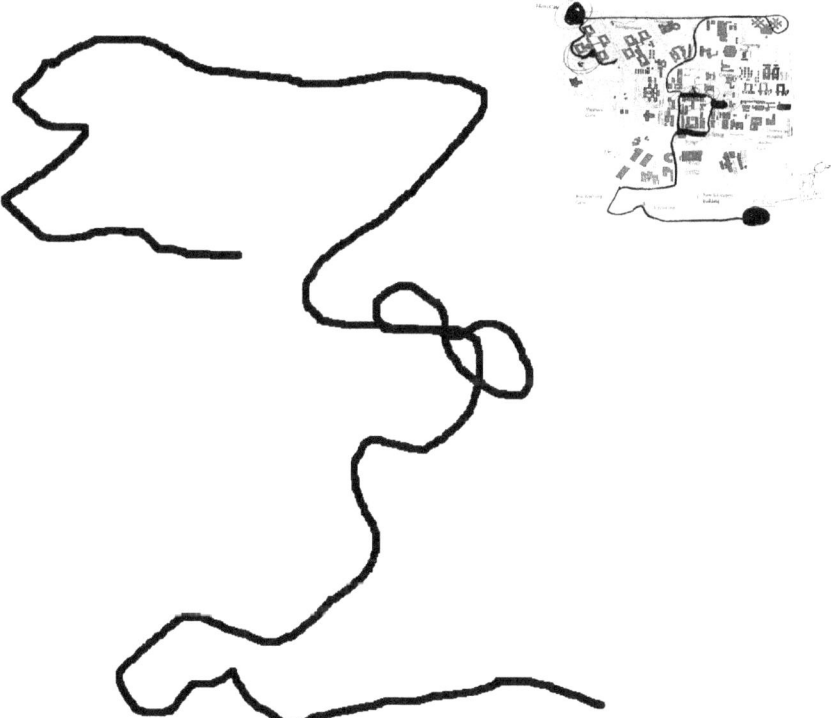

Figure 21 The line we walked, 2019.
Digital drawing, Frans Kruger.

The cartography in Chapter 6 (see Figure 20) guided us to draw this line as we followed the nodes in the narrative that connect to the space.

7.3 A Place that Hurts

We started our walk at Shimla Park, the first node on our line. In almost all the interviews we did with educators at the UFS, this space emerged as an affective space of pain, confusion and anger due to the events that had played out here in 2016 (Dick et al. 2019). It emerged from the story told by Pinkovski and Daisy, of the night and days after the event (Section 3.2); also in Lizzy and Jolene's disillusionment (6.2.2), Book's becoming (6.2.3) and finally Elize and Dan's struggles, trauma and arrest (6.2.7).

We thought of Shimla Park as a node, or a place where many lines meet, many narratives crossed, and thus it become part of our walking. As we approached Shimla Park, we were met by two refrains: first, the wind that drowned out our

Figure 22 A place that hurts, 2019.
Photograph, Marguerite Müller.

conversation and second, a *kiewiet* (a plover) that tried to change our course – and *warn* us not to enter its territory.

We stopped at a noticeboard that warned us: Right of admission reserved. Enter at own risk.

What we hear is the wind and the *kiewiet*. What we see is the fence and what we think about is territory, manliness, nationalism and capitalism. How are these this folded into this space? How is it folded into us? We wonder about this when one of us steps on a devils thorn. Ouch!

The space that hurts is a space where different stories and histories were negotiated. A multiplicity of trajectories and flows met at this node, and a problematic relationality, an imbalance of power relations, played out at Shimla Park. Do affects of anger, humiliation and fear seep into the grass of the sports field after a while? What happens to a space where the terms of the fair construction of equal relations were irrevocably violated? We become wounded. Some affective incidents are more difficult to counter-actualize than others. Being worthy of what happens to us becomes difficult in a space where injustice and fear hovers in the air for too long.

7.4 A Leak in the Surface

Water is bubbling out of the ground and leaking onto the dry earth. Does anyone know about this leak? This drought is scary; we should report the leak.

We talk about water a lot – or at least about the lack of water, about the drought. The bird sounds intermingle with a group of passing joggers. We walk past the construction site where a new building is leaking onto the surface – right next to the Education Building, another node in the narrative, where we start writing the book in Marguerite's office (Section 2.1). Beep beep beep… the sound of a forklift. No tuition fees means more students and the need for bigger buildings.

7.5 Crossing a Bridge

Memory is like a bridge between then and now. The bridge is also a node in the narrative and the symbol of a bridge also emerged in Lebo's narrative (Section 5.4.2).

As we cross the Thakaneng Bridge (the food court), we remember the day after Shimla Park as a single dot on the line where the past and present collided – and the future was created in the past. The dot shows chaos and the dot shows order. We are on a bridge between the two.

Figure 23 Then and later, 2016 and 2019.
Photographs, Marguerite Müller.

Where the name of Steve Biko[1] used to be spray-painted on a tree in the past became the Steve Biko Building in the present – the space that Jolene remembers as somewhere she did not have a voice (Section 6.2.2).

7.6 A Dot on the Line

We change course. We visit a site that is a memorial to and remembrance of a friend who passed away a few years ago. Our affective connection to the

More than Human 131

Figure 24 Steve Biko House, 2016 and 2019.
Photographs, Marguerite Müller.

space draws us on a different line and makes us change course. *Ongemagtigde toegang verbode* (unauthorized entry forbidden) makes us think of the territories of the living and the dead – our inability to have access to the person who passed away – yet, in the space is a residue of her presence, a physical presence in the drawing and an affective presence in our memories and loss.

We walk to the artist Willem Boshoff's *Thinking Stone*,[2] a black granite rock that was taken from deep inside the earth, and which was placed in the vicinity of where Steyn's statue used to stand (see Section 5.1). We sit on the massive rock while sliding our fingers over the marks that resemble prehistoric rock engravings. What does it mean? Its dark solidity means it rests like a giant paperweight on the surface of our line. In Chapter 5 (5.4.3), we reported on the remembrances of Book and Lebo of events that took place before and after

Figure 25 A dot on the line, 2019.
Photograph, Marguerite Müller. Photograph of artwork by Dot Vermeulen, "Collect and Reject" (2013).

the Reitz incident, events that took place on the Red Square. What kind of conversations would Steyn have had with the thinking stone?

Behind the stone lies the main building, its large form framed by the blue of the Bloemfontein sky. From there, we walk to a newly installed patch of plastic green grass – the drought and water scarcity lead to the demise of the 'real' lawn that used to cover this space. We feel the plastic grass beneath our bare feet – it looks nice and feels soft, but it is warm.

7.7 Empty Space Full of Memories

In the days after Shimla Park, the protesters removed the statue of C. R. Swart. Riley referred to the significance of symbols and statues (Section 6.2.2), which emerged again at the removal of Steyn's statue (Section 6.2.10). The silent march (Section 5.1) started on the Red Square, where Steyn's statue had stood at the time.

Figure 26 *Thinking Stone*, 2011.
Installation, Willem Boshoff. Belfast black granite, 480 × 335 × 120 cm. University of the Free State Art Collection. Images courtesy of the UFS.

The space where C. R. Swart used to sit is now empty. All traces of him are gone. The emptiness is filled with memories of events that took place on this campus. But the space is empty. The names have changed, from C. R. Swart to Robert Sobukwe Law School to Equitas.

A memory (Müller 2017, 217–18):

> Early morning quiet
> autumn air
> strolling past the same spot
> where CR Swart is lying

> motionless in the pond
> Staring up at the crisp Bloemfontein blue
> Dry leaves rustle in the trees
> Shhhh
> The stone slab where he used to rest
> Still erect
> like a grave stone
> Someone is painting over the fresh graffiti on a nearby wall
> SOBUKWE LAW SCHOOL is slowly disappearing
> Under a new coat of paint
> Renaming
> Erasing
> Claiming

We reach the main gate and the Madelief residence where Liezl worked and lived for six years. This is another affective node on our line, where several narratives and events connect. In Section 3.2, Liezl described her encounter the protesters on her *stoep*, and Lebo (5.4.3) shared wine with colleagues on the Madelief residence head's *stoep* to debrief after the Reitz incident. Elize and Dan recalled incidents of police brutality, unrest and chaos (6.2.7) there after Shimla Park. The #FeesMustFall protests also started at this node.

Liezl and Marguerite:
the warm concrete,
the displaced guardhouse,
the fence that was flattened by a tree,
only recently so that the scent of freshly cut pine lingers as we walk past.
The warm sun is beating down on us.

We pass the Agriculture Building and its Cartesian subject.
A dead office plant is looking sadly from its window.
We come to a standstill at the newly constructed graffiti wall.

Marguerite: 'And yet, if everything is moving, where is here?' (Massey 2005, 138).
Liezl: 'If there are no fixed points then where is here?' (Massey 2005, 138).
   And are we here, now?
Frans:

> Space and time, together, [is] the outcome of this multiple becoming.
> Then 'here' is no more (and no less) than our encounter, and what is

Figure 27 Barbed wire, 2019.
Photograph, Marguerite Müller.

made of it. It is, irretrievably, here and now. It won't be the same 'here' when it is no longer now. 'Here' is where spatial narratives meet up or form configurations, conjunctures of trajectories which have their own temporalities. … 'Here' is an intertwining of histories in which the spatiality of those histories (their then as well as their here) is inescapably entangled. The interconnections themselves are part of the construction of identity (Massey 2005, 139).

Figure 28 Cartesian subject? 2019.
Photograph, Marguerite Müller.

7.8 Copying the Gesture

In walking a line through this space, we were caught between doing and describing. The narratives of affective incidents in this space gave us a line – the stories were agents that showed us where to go. As we walked through the space physically, we experienced the collision between past and present – the physicality of the present was filled with affect that flowed from the narratives of the past.

The relational nature of critical arts-based pedagogies and research provides opportunities to think-through and become-with aesthetic encounters in ways that bypass the limits and possibilities of normative, logocentric and dominant disciplines and discourses within institutions of higher education. We pay specific attention to subjectivity in relation to place and the posthuman entanglements that constitute it. To do this, we start by considering how the concept of artfulness (Manning 2014) may inform inquiry-for-practice and inquiry-as-practice. Manning suggests that arts-based research 'proposes concrete assemblages for rethinking the very question of what is at stake in pedagogy, in practice, and in collective experimentation' (Manning 2015, 53). Similarly, Manning draws on Mazzei's insights into how arts-based research can be used to read data defractively (Barad 2003): 'A diffractive reading of data through multiple theoretical insights moves qualitative analysis away from habitual normative readings (e.g., coding) toward a diffractive reading that spreads thought and meaning in unpredictable and productive emergences' (Mazzei 2014, 742). We thought of our walking as one would think of the line drawn by a pencil. As the line extends, it follows the path or plan of the artist, but, at the same time, it produces new possibilities or productive and unpredictable encounters that could not be planned. Art helps us to respond to the reserve, as the line cannot exist without it. In this way, the creation of an artwork is a negotiated encounter between human and non-human actors.

In this chapter, we walked into an encounter with place and space, as non-human participants in our inquiry. We conceptualized place as assembled and affective, consisting of nonhuman entanglements that continuously become-other through their interactions. We proposed that exploring such entanglements and the becomings they produce may create openings for critically considering educator subjectivity as it finds expression within a specific place and a specific time.

We copied the gesture of the line. The space we walked through acted as the reserve. The copying of the gesture was our way of attuning to form-giving – the creative force of making meaning with our minds and bodies at the same time. We were hot and tired, and we felt the physicality of the 'interview' made us think differently about the narrative, the line and the reserve. We heard refrains of birds, water and wind. We also heard the noises of construction and conversations. In walking the line, we were not describing, but making sense and thinking of the past in the present and the future.

7.9 Walking, Looking and Listening

In this chapter, we showed how place and space can become participants in research inquiry. We drew on narratives as more-than-human agents that guided our inquiry. Walking and arts-based inquiry was used to guide intra-action (Barad 2003) with the place and space of the wound. We walked a line through a reserve and remembered that 'even when no one is visiting a story it is living … Narratives become descriptions of particular complex possibilities for future being that exist whether or not they are actualized. Their possibility influences the present – gives the present its form' (Rosiek and Snyder 2018, 9). Below, we outline our process of encountering place and space through walking.

How to encounter the more-than-human in narrative form

- Listen to the narratives.
- Find the nodes on the narrative map, this is where the intensities and the affect connect the story to the space.

Figure 29 A new wall, 2019.
Photograph, Marguerite Müller.

- 'Interview' the space by listening, looking and feeling (pay attention).
- Take photos, record sound, make drawings.

Questions

- What is the space telling us?
- What is the space asking of us?
- What does space, as a research participant, make possible in a post-qualitative inquiry?
- How does space shape subjectivity?
- How does subjectivity shape space?

8

We Are Not Statues: Becoming with Hope and Uncertainty

8.1 The End of the Line

With this chapter, we reach the end of a line. The end of a line always has the potential to extend. So, let's rather think of this as a pause. We wrote this book to explore how our personal experiences in this context shaped our professional identities. Our aim was to gain insight into educator subjectivity during a time of social change in the South African higher education landscape. We set out on a journey to tell a story and we were conscious that the story we would tell has many points of entry: a rhizomatic adventure. The snapshot we offered gives a glimpse into the experiences of educators in a specific time and place. Now, at the end of the line, we need to re-emphasize that this is just a snapshot and nothing more. This snapshot allows for an explorative discussion on educator subjectivity in higher education. In this book, we experimented with the theoretical concepts of Deleuze and Guatari along with arts-based, narrative and post-qualitative inquiry to engage educator subjectivity during a time of social change. We plugged the concepts into our own lives the narratives of participants and the space of the UFS to find out how the one was affected and changed by the other in our affective and agentic research assemblage. This 'worlding' and 'research-making' endeavour enabled us to explore 'theorizing as practice' (Gale 2020), while employing experimental research and a writing style that focused on creation and exploration rather than repetition and representation. In this way, we wanted to share the dynamism of social change and transformation, and educator subjectivity as processual and always already becoming-with-the-other.

In a context of decolonization, we have to ask critical questions about the production of knowledge, how we represent that knowledge and how we are embedded in both the process of and its expression: how it is created, for whom, by whom and to what purpose. We also critically engaged with processes of educator subjectification during a time of decolonization, transformation and rapid change. Our engagement with belonging and place is located in the assemblage and the wound. The concepts of the assembled subject and the wound as event allowed us to understand subjectivity as an emerging rhizomatic adventure rather than a centred or rational subject. We are not statues. Our exploration has helped us understand that we need to pay attention to our own collective becomings. Paying attention might help us to receive strange gifts, such as uncertainty, and that, in turn, can help us stay with the predicament or, in the words of Haraway (2016), 'staying with the trouble'. It is our task to stay with the wound and to revisit the event. But each visit and each counter-actualization is different and offers a new point of entry. Every time we tell a story, we change. The story is an agentic force that guides our becomings and shows us how the future might be different; how we might be different in the future. In this book, we resisted giving final answers, or drawing conclusions. We embraced the unexpected and creative force that allowed us to embrace our journey of becoming educators as a never-ending adventure.

8.2 Looking Forward Is Looking Back

This is not the end of the line; instead, it is the moment where the line disappears from our view and we pause to look back at how we go from here.

In Chapter 1, 'If You Want to Go Far, Go Together: An Introduction, we set the scene for this book. We explained that the book exists in a specific context and we offered a snapshot of a moment in time and place. We explained how we think of educator subjectivity as processual and as by-products of processes of subjectification. The assembled subject and the wound are concepts that allow us to processually understand how things work, rather than what the thing is. The aim of this book was to use theory and methodology to create new and authentic ways of thinking about professional educator subjectivity in relation to rapid social change. We conceptualized educator subjectivity along a personal/professional continuum. Throughout the book, we showed the entangled expression of professional and personal experience in the higher education context. The question we started with was, how can we use theory and methodology to think differently about educator subjectivity during a time of rapid change? Theory and method helped us to respond to the context and events of life.

In Chapter 2, 'Assembling Roots and Writing a Book: Theory and Methodology Meet', we used dialogue to sketch our collaborative process of working, thinking and writing together. The dialogues serve as a tool to unpack the theoretical and methodological angles of this book, and how these approaches might contribute to a project of decolonization in higher education. With Chapter 2 we initiated a discussion of how theory and methodology might shape research into educator subjectivity and social change in higher education by looking at Deleuze and Guattari's figurations of assemblage, affect, rhizome, becoming and the use of cartography. We also discussed how arts-based and post-qualitative inquiry could help us to explore educator subjectivity. In Chapter 2 (Section 2.4) we also worked with the question of how we could write together. Using our own subjectivities as experimental laboratories, we gathered the methodological and theoretical tools that made the writing process possible. In Section 8.2, we echo this process and moved the setting of the dialogue from physical or actual spaces of Chapter 2 (office, campus, coffee shop, gallery) to virtual spaces in Chapter 8 (video chat meeting).

In Chapter 3, 'A Tale of the Assembled Subject: Exploring Whiteness', we used our own assembled subjectivities to create a performative narrative. We created a non-linear narrative of how our multiple educator identities unfold against the backdrop of personal and professional experiences. The performative text showed how subjectivity, as a multiplicity, could be used to explore its affective connections. By positioning whiteness as one aspect of the assembled subject, we sought to understand and trouble essentialized identities and demonstrate subjectivity as multiple and emergent. Our aim here was to complicate one-dimensional notions of identity and subjectivity and explore its affective connections by using a lens of whiteness to unpack our positionality in the context. The aim of the chapter is to look at how performative writing could be used to express complexity of research on educator subjectivity.

In Chapter 4, 'Finding What You Have Not Yet Lost: An Affective Inquiry into Educator Subjectivity', we explored how arts-based and post-qualitative inquiry can expand our understanding of educator subjectivity as affective and connected. Here, we explained our process of creating research encounters and interpreting these into a research text. The chapter demonstrates how the theory and methodology we employed made it possible to conceptualize educator identity as a multiplicity. Through the use of affect, we demonstrated the possibilities of a personal/professional educator identity continuum in education for social change. In this chapter, we aimed to create a guide for researchers who would like to use arts-based inquiry.

Chapter 5, 'To Not be Unworthy of What Happens to Us, We Go to the Morgues Ourselves: Wounded Becomings', employed a collective biography of women that explores and interrogates the wound-event as becoming. In this chapter, we used Deleuze's philosophy of the wound-event to understand subjectivity, as expressed through memory, as an assembled and affective 'event' rather than a fixed entity. The visual autobiographical narratives of educators are created as a response to the question, Who are we now and how did we get here? In this way, we sought to collaboratively make connections between our experiences and the experiences of others, resulting in a memory assemblage. Through the memory assemblage, we sought to explore subjectivity as a multiplicity in a visual way. Memory has the potential to form a positive feedback loop into professional praxis, which helps us to explore the personal/profession continuum. Here, our arts-based inquiry connected with the act of counter-actualization to explore the becomings of educators.

Chapter 6, 'Can You Please Come Back Later? A Cartography of Becoming Educators', presented a cartography of becoming educators. Here, we used non-linear time to play with the idea of becoming educators. We specifically used the narratives of students who had become educators during a time of rapid social change in higher education in South Africa. By conflating the personal/professional educator identity binary, we hope to show ways of thinking creatively through social change and transformation. The chapter used cartography to plug and connect narratives into each other. This entangled expression of becoming shows how educator subjectivity develops through disruption and encounter. This process is non-linear and non-causal and highlights the value of moving away from common-sense notions of time and space.

In Chapter 7, 'More than Human: An Exploration of the Entanglement of Educator Subjectivity and Space', we turned to space as a research participant. We used narratives, as agents, to guide us through the space. In keeping with the theoretical underpinnings presented in the preceding chapters, place was conceptualized as assembled and affective, consisting of networks of human and non-human actors that continuously become-other as they come into relation with one another. It is envisioned that exploring these relations, and the becomings they produce, will provide openings to critically consider personal/professional educator identity in terms of its materiality as it finds expression within a specific place. We aimed to show how walking as transformative pedagogy can help us consider the material and affective aspects of the recent calls for transformation, social change and decolonization at higher education institutions in South Africa.

Chapter 8, 'We Are not Statues: Becoming with Hope and Uncertainty', serves as the conclusion of this book. This chapter presents a reflection exercise on what theory and methodology made possible for our research on educator subjectivity. We reflect on how different chapters form a research assemblage. The exploration in previous chapters lead us to think about how hope and uncertainty inform becoming of educators during a time of rapid social change.

8.3 A Video Chat Meeting: New Subjectivities, Assemblages and Wounds

So many strange things have passed before me in those timeless moments that fall into one's life as if from the moon, when one no longer has any idea how old one is or how young one will yet be (Nietzsche 1968, 534).

Liezl: August 2020. I am sitting in my sister's house in Pretoria. Two weeks ago, I had packed up my flat in Bloemfontein and relocated to be closer to family. A panic attack, which was probably caused by a Skype reading group session, the stress of packing up and moving, a midlife crisis accompanied by an existential crisis followed by a deep depression, combined with low serotonin and oxytocin levels due to a three-year postdoctoral self-isolation stint, plus a ticking biological clock, amidst a global pandemic, and a looming book deadline… well, I lost track of the apparent 'causes' of the panic attack. My point being the panic attack accelerated the move to Pretoria and provided me with the help and assistance I needed from friends and family. The panic has been attacking me, quite frankly, since March, when the epidemic started in South Africa. Or it may have been there long before March, perhaps since Shimla Park? Since the incident on my *stoep*? Since my friend Dot died in a car accident years ago (Section 7.6)? Or maybe even since childhood? A perpetual state of anxiety brought about by the perception of the future as dangerous and the world as threatening? 'It's been a long time comin'', Bruce Springsteen sings, 'but now it's here'.

I get a message:
Marguerite Muller is inviting you to a scheduled video chat meeting.
Topic: My Meeting
Time: Aug 28, 2020 09:30 AM Johannesburg

Join video chat meeting

https://ufs.Video Chat.us/j/94174895737?pwd=WSVideo Chatmeetingassemblagemultiplicity

Figure 30 Video chat meeting.
Screenshot.

> **Book:** Paradoxical, isn't it, that COVID-19 made the connections with loved ones possible as well as movement, growth, change and transformation that were unsuitable or unthinkable for the pre-COVID, isolated self, insisting on and believing in independence and self-sustainability?

> **Marguerite:** So, COVID and the lockdown closed certain well-trodden paths. We had to follow new paths. We had to open new doors. The paradox of crisis is that it forced us to create new ways of engaging, meeting and new ways to enter into dialogue with the world.

> **Book:** 'Paradoxes matter', Williams (2008, 25) writes, 'because they reveal limits within systems and require passages beyond internal rules of validity and consistency. Thought moves on and connects through paradox … paradox bears its solutions while affirming their temporary and unsatisfactory nature.

Liezl: It took a national lockdown to get me out of my own self-inflicted lockdown. At this stage, I am convinced that COVID-19 saved me from myself: an unsustainable trajectory that was interrupted by an unpredictable, paradoxical chance encounter. My subjectivity, as affective assemblage and as event, was a by-product of several encounters, events, affective connections with human and non-human elements, while my experience of the past and thoughts about the future are all processes that co-created my subjectivity as by-product of these flows and movements. I am a multiplicity and I am never alone. The 'I' becomes an illusion, and all that remains are processes, intensities, temporality, affects and flows. Movement, transformation and change. The *eventfulness* (Gale 2020) of life.

Book: Massumi (2002a, 214) highlights the role of affect and how it connects us (because we are all but processes and events, aren't we?):

the way we live … is always entirely *embodied,* and that is never entirely personal – it's never all contained in our emotions and conscious thoughts. That's a way of saying it's not just about us, in isolation. In affect, we are never alone. That's because affects in Spinoza's definition are basically ways of *connecting*, to others and to other situations. With intensified affect comes a stronger sense of embeddedness in a larger field of life – a heightened sense of belonging, with other people and to other places.

Liezl: What this implies is that the Reitz incident, Shimla Park, the event of apartheid, the blowing wind in Bloemfontein, childhood memories, dreams about the future, fear of the future, the breakfast that we ate that morning, the drawings that were done in workshops, tears, agony, laughter, this present moment while we are meeting on video chat, sitting at my sister's dinner table feeling unhinged, the Free State dust, colonialism, love, the joys of motherhood and the pain of loss – all of these participated in the becomings of subjectivity.

Marguerite: That brings us back to the aim of the book. Our aim in this book was to trouble educator identity in order to create new ways of thinking about professional educator identity in relation to rapid social change within the context of higher education in South Africa. By troubling educator identity, we troubled a static notion of our own identities. We wanted to evoke affective connections from the reader; we had to ask ourselves how the reader can affectively connect with the narratives and becomings of educators. And what kind of becomings can these intensive, affected connections make possible? Our experimental writing and research style aimed to proliferate the possible connections that can be made. To make connections is to experiment, and experimentation is becoming, and becoming and change is the stuff that transformation is made of. But how does this link to the theory and concepts we used?

Book: Theoretically, several key Deleuzian/Deleuzoguattarian concepts helped Marguerite and Liezl to proceed with an experimental methodology in their quest to trouble educator identity in a time of rapid social change; these concepts are the affect, assemblage, cartography, rhizome and the event. These concepts make a processual notion of subjectivity as relational and in flux, always changing, possible. While the assemblage with its nodes and endless possibility of rhizomatic connections makes a spatial, relational and affective understanding of subjectivity possible, the notion of subjectivity as eventful brings a temporal, common sense and non-causal dimension to how they perceive subjectivation processes. These concepts make it possible to think of subjectivity as the by-product of heterogeneous (human and more-than-human) elements, affective incidents, processes, flows and intensities, and a temporality that privileges randomness, chance and an openness to the future. And, to think differently about educator subjectivity, Marguerite and Liezl aimed to open up new avenues of becomings and different, authentic ways of doing research about these becomings.

Liezl: And these new avenues of becoming can only emerge through fundamental encounters with and in the world (Deleuze 2004b, 176), which are problems that 'force[s] us to think'. The most important characteristics of a fundamental encounter is that it can only be sensed and not recognized. According to Deleuze, recognition depends on identity thinking and representation. A fundamental encounter pushes thinking beyond common sense and categorical thinking, towards the new, that which can only be sensed, that is, the imperceptible. The objective is thus not solutions and answers but experiencing a new order that a confrontation with a problem makes possible (Williams 2013, 128–9).

Marguerite: So, the radically new can only come about if we can stop the urge to categorize and classify the unfamiliar that we encounter?

Liezl: Yes. If we can begin to think beyond the obsession to categorize, classify and judge, the new might have the opportunity to reveal itself. Deleuze blames the dogmatic image of thought for this. In the dogmatic image of thought, recognition operates as the faculty that validates the existence of something. Recognition is the one faculty that presupposes the other faculties, and on which the other faculties rely. 'We sense *this* because we recognize it. We understand *that* because we recognize it' (Williams 2013, 125–6). However, recognition doesn't allow for something new to enter the world; according to this line of thinking, the novel and new can only be understood – hence recognized as existent – in terms of the known. Only that which is already *known* can be *recognized* and *acknowledged* as *existent/existing*, after which it will be categorized and be made predictable.

Marguerite: Is this how identity thinking functions?

Liezl: Indeed. Deleuze criticizes this common-sense understanding of recognition by claiming that recognition breaks difference and 'the new' into something that has already been recognized and hence already known. This conservative commitment of philosophy to recognition doesn't leave space for difference-in-itself, which is the new that can't be recognized, identified or resembled; hence, becoming (Williams 2013, 126–7, 180–3; Deleuze 2004b, xiv–xv). Categorical thinking limits *how* and *what* the subject knows and the ways in which *others* can know the subject are equally limited; it prevents the subject from becoming something different than the category she has been allocated to and also prevents her from knowing the world in its uncategorical multiplicity of sensations and affects (Williams 2013, 128).

Marguerite: All of this makes sense, Liezl. It is important, however, to emphasize that, in the process that we encounter 'the new' and unknown, people become afraid. And at the heart of this novelty, possibility and newness lies uncertainty. And uncertainty – and becoming – can be daunting. To write Book, we used a post-qualitative methodology that embraces uncertainty and experimentation by necessity. The 'success' of our methodology thus relied on how willing we were to embrace uncertainty and the unknown. On top of this, we wrote this book during a time of acute uncertainty and social change – not only did we engage with social and political transformation, but we also found ourselves in the midst of a global pandemic. Uncertainty was rife and everywhere.

Liezl: Yes, I agree. We basically wrote this book with the help of uncertainty; uncertainty as a research participant! ☺ The radically new, the unknown and uncertainty, however, fill most people with fear and anxiety. Although we are keen on notions of development, transformation, creativity and progress, human beings tend to be overwhelmed by the uncontainable, unpredictable and unstable aspects of societal change and transformation. We want to keep the anxiety of the not-yet-known at bay; chance, randomness and lack of control trigger fearful and limiting reactions. So, how do we open ourselves up for the radically new, randomness, chance and creativity if these notions make us anxious? How do we allow for the new to be born? (Grosz 1999, 15).

Book:

Predictable, measured, regulated transformation changes under specifiable conditions and with determinate effects seem a readily presumed social prerequisite; upheaval, the eruption of the event and the emergence of new alignments unpredicted within old networks threaten to reverse all gains, to position progress on the edge of an abyss, to place chaos at the heart of regulation and orderly development. *How is it possible to revel and delight in the indeterminacy of the future without raising the kind of panic and defensive counterreactions that surround the attempts of the old to contain the new, to predict, anticipate, and incorporate the new within its already existing frameworks* (Grosz 1999, 16) (emphasis added)?

Marguerite: This question is also applicable to our research and aligns with our arts-based and experimental research methodology. How do we allow for the future to unfold, for the radically new to emerge, if we are holding on too tightly to the predictable, the containable and desire to control the future? Answer: We need to challenge the dominant ways of knowing that is imbedded in colonial logic – the causal and the statistical – as these methods of knowledge production are not equipped to conceive of or to imagine the radically new. New ways of knowing, which allow for the absolutely new to emerge and that allow the future to be open and rife with endless possibilities, should be explored (Grosz 1999, 21). How do we remain open to these possibilities? How do we create alternatives to deterministic, limiting and constraining research approaches in education?

Liezl: To allow for new ways of being and becoming, we have to create alternatives to the deterministic approach to the future that is dominated by scientific predictability. To surrender to the open-endedness of the future and to allow for any event to play out, privilege notions of chance, randomness and unpredictability; the future as trajectory or direction without destination, to think of movement as rhizomatic rather than as movement as prediction (Grosz 1999, 18).

This endeavour of exploration can be guided by a focus on possibility, rather than on predictability (Stengers 2002).

Marguerite: And during challenging times, such as we are currently experiencing due to COVID-19, it's especially necessary to choose for possibility against probability. Hope, Stengers writes, is to be able to define the difference between possibility and probability. There are so many reasons to give up the hope for a better future and to give in to despair. To rather choose for a creative mode of being and knowing is to resist this seemingly all-engulfing despair. To create possibilities against a deterministic, causal and 'common sense' logic of probability is what it means to truly *think*.

Book: Stenger's notion of hope as the creation of possibilities aligns with the Deleuzoguattarian rhizomatic image of thought, which provides us with an alternative to the rational, arboreal traditional image of thought (Deleuze and Guattari 2008), which informed our research methodology; we choose, instead, to be curious about the unknown rather than to be overwhelmed by fear. What will we find on this journey? Which unfamiliar elements will emerge that we could not have predicted? What are the unexpected connections that were made?

Marguerite: Book, you have become part of our assemblage. This gives me hope. The other is just another self. Liezl, what do we hope for, with Book?

Liezl: Although it is true that evidence-based research is necessary and much needed in some areas, it is also true that a deterministic, evidence-based methodology and worldview will inhibit the absolutely new ways of becoming and being. To hope, Lingis (2002, 23) avers, is to break with the past and to go *against* the evidence provided towards the open-endedness of the future. We need hope, especially when the present is too unbearable to endure. This understanding of hope as a break from the past indicates a discontinuity in time – a line of flight appears out of nowhere, making new connections, possibilities and futures possible.

Marguerite: So, hope is like a gift. You accept it even before you have opened it or know what it is?

Liezl: Yes, hope is discontinuous, not evidence-based, hope for the new to be born. 'Hope is to hope that things can be born in your life' (Lingis 2002, 41). 'It does not come out of what went before, but *in spite of* what went before' (Lingis 2002, 24; emphasis added). One can also argue for a more immediate, in-the-moment hopefulness rather than perceiving hope as something that will happen one day in the future. Such an utopian view can also be debilitating, and Lingis and Massumi suggest a shift from hope to a Spinozian understanding of joy where joy is something that we experience in the now, in the moment, and which infects our bodies, here and now. In this sense, then we move into the future joyfully, while staying in the here and now, focused on what a body can do and how bodies can become more alive by affecting and being affected by one another. Joy increases the capacity to connect, to act and to become (Deleuze and Guattari 2008; Massumi 2002b; Spinoza 1957). The importance of hope and joy in our academic and research endeavours are thus crucial, especially during seemingly hopeless times of change.

Marguerite:
having fun seriously matters
and playfully thinking
how to create
gives you new answers
to questions you did not think to ask
having fun seriously
matters
and that finding joy
in discovery of difficult things
helps
a lot
because research
is not a recipe
at all
but it is a risky and exciting
journey
into the unknown
where unexpected things await. (Muller, 2020)

Liezl: We, as researchers, should explore the new and its possibilities, undeterred by the overwhelming counter-arguments conducted in favour of misfortune. A joyful, hopeful mindset is especially necessary when one proceeds experimentally and collaboratively (Lingis 2002, 24); to avoid being overwhelmed by the unknown, a curiosity about what can be found is quite helpful. This hopeful, joyful curiosity is a great mindset to have, especially when you collaborate with a colleague! This makes the exploration of unpredictable encounters and connects possible. To hope is to have courage. Laughter 'breaks open another time' (Lingis 2002, 25). In this sense, counter-actualization and how we rework our stories and experiences through narratives and arts can be read as hopeful endeavours, as this is also a way of embracing the eventfulness of our lives as hopeful. To counter-actualize our experiences is a hopeful endeavour and this creates a discontinuity in time and makes new trajectories of becomings possible.

Uncertainty joins the video chat meeting.

It's commonsensical to give preference to evidence, to predictability. Statistics don't lie. Surely it's silly to cultivate unrealistic hope, joy and expectations during these highly precarious times. How paradoxical and irrational. Why would one want to follow such a counter-intuitive research approach? Be sensible, women!

Becoming joins the video chat meeting.

We can answer that only by embracing the paradoxical and the uncertain, the affective and irrational, we can allow for the radically new to appear; it is this complex 'othertimeliness' and anxiety that lies at the heart of becoming, transformation and change. When we are confronted with something that can be neither recognized nor categorized, we can choose to become either anxious and overwhelmed by the radically new or we can choose to explore the unknown and the new and decide to be curious about the uncertainty we are faced with. Uncertainty, Massumi (2002a, 211) avers, can be empowering because it can bring what he calls 'a margin of manoeuvrability' to a situation, which allows for experimentation, and for a 'try and see what happens' attitude rather than a focus on success or failure. This brings potential to a situation.

- **Uncertainty:** '[Uncertainty] might force you to find a margin, a manoeuvre you didn't know you had, and couldn't have just thought your way into. It can change you, expand you. That's what being alive is all about' (Massumi 2002a, 217).
- **Marguerite:** So, uncertainty is part of the assemblage of educator subjectivity during rapid social change. It is part of the flows of intensities that shape us. We need to embrace uncertainty with innovation and creation instead of trying to avoid it.

Deleuze joins the video chat meeting.

But when substantives and adjectives begin to dissolve and when the names of pause and rest are carried away by the verbs of pure becoming and slide into the language of events, all identity disappears from the self, the world and God. This is the test of *savoir* (to know) and recitation, which strips Alice of her identity. In it words may go awry, being obliquely swept away by the verbs. It is as if events enjoyed an irreality which is communicated through language to the savoir and to persons. For personal uncertainty is not a doubt foreign to what is happening but rather an objective structure of the event itself, insofar as it moves in two directions at once and insofar as it fragments the subject following this double direction. Paradox is initially that which destroys good sense as the only direction, but it is also that which destroys common sense as the assignation of fixed identities (Deleuze 1990, 3).

Liezl: So, we have to become undone in order to become? So, instead of shutting uncertainty out, we see it as the indicator that there are now possibilities of becoming – previously unseen, hidden.

Book: Massumi uses the concept of affect, and affect as virtuality, to talk about a margin of manoeuvrability, and he uses affect as a way to indicate hope.

One of the reasons it's such an important concept for me is because it explains why focusing on the next experimental step rather than the big utopian picture isn't really settling for less. It's not exactly going for more, either. It's rather like being right where you are – more intensely (Massumi 2002a, 217).

Marguerite: It is like staying with the predicament and staying with the trouble?

Liezl: Absolutely. 'Staying with the trouble requires learning to be truly present … as mortal critters entwined in myriad unfinished configurations of places, times, matters and meanings' (Haraway 2016, 1).

Book: Williams argues that uncertainty doesn't necessarily have to be a negative, and brings an element of experimentation, provided we can focus on the possibility and potential it brings, rather than be overwhelmed by fear about what is not certain:

Uncertainty, in the multiplication of perspectives on a reality itself multiple and always changing, is far from negative if accompanied by a constant and generous experimentation – as in the uncertainty of a child in the presence of an unfamiliar object and perceptions. What ought we to prefer: accurate, complicated and manifold enquiries or the banishment of the best tools for such enquiries because they do not favour the passing and already faded uncertainties of restricted groups (Williams 2008, 206)?

Marguerite: Uncertainty, in this sense, is almost like curiosity? It invites us to interact with that which we don't know. How does uncertainty link to educator subjectivity?

Liezl: Yes! To approach uncertainty with an experimental and playful approach can allow for more options and possibilities to emerge in a given situation. During times of uncertainty, we can create space, perspectives and movement for ourselves to ensure we react in a way that 'brings the maximum potential and connection to the situation (Williams 2008, 218). Because, how we react in times of uncertainty has ethical implications, seeing that ethics are pragmatic and situational and take place between people (Williams 2008, 218)). And if we follow a Spinozian ethics when we are faced with uncertainty, we should do whatever optimizes affection, connection and becoming-together, becoming other. In this sense, an ethical situation is one that refuses to be inhibited by the fear of uncertainty; the ethical action would be the action that enhances becoming. So how does this link to educator subjectivity in a time of social change? The implication is that if you are an educator, your becoming is proliferated or deterred by *how* you *react* to the flux and flow of intensities and affects that affect you while you find yourself in the context of social change and transformation. As an educator, you can choose how you react to the challenges you are confronted with: will you close yourself down, try to hold on to the illusion of stability and essentialist notions of yourself? Will you resist the demands of change and shy away from opportunities to break out of an old, outdated mould and mode of being? Or will you embrace the challenges of change, uncertainty and the unknown? Will you open yourself up to things beyond and out of your comfort zone, new connections that will make new ways of being and becoming possible?

Marguerite: Yes. This links to how do we do research in ways that allow for new subjectivities to emerge, and the emergence of new processes of subjectification demands counter-intuitive notions of spatiality and temporality. In this book, we demonstrated what research infused by time as non-linear and space as open and always changing, might result in.

Book:

> The future is never fixed and always lives within the unexpected notyetness of each new encounter. In the constant processualism of practice, there is a need 'to be willing to surprise yourself writing things you didn't think you thought. Letting examples burgeon requires using inattention as a writing tool' (Gale 2020, 304).

Marguerite: Because it is only through uncertainty, randomness and chance that different trajectories of becomings and, may we even say, better futures might be possible as alternatives to the status quo. Common sense and traditional ways of thinking are not sufficient anymore. Reality is changing constantly and to keep up with the times, we can't afford to create fictions that we believe in too strongly. We need manoeuvrability, movement and experimentation and have to focus on processes, events and transformations. Thus, it's imperative that we give privilege to notions of randomness and chance and embrace understandings of time and subjectivity that privileges the non-linear and non-causal (Grosz 1999, 4).

Choir of voices: Okay, but what are the practical implications of all of this, you might ask? How does one live a meaningful life amidst the chaos and uncertainty at the heart of transformation and rapid social change? How can we proceed to do meaningful research when we are not comforted by the illusion of control, certainty, statistics and causality?

Liezl: While I was staying with my sister and her family during the national lockdown, my three-year-old niece watched *Frozen 2* on repeat, day in and day out. By the time the lockdown was lifted, all the adults in the house who had worked from home to the beat of the *Frozen* songs titled *Into the unknown, Just do the next right thing* and *Let it go* (from *Frozen 1*, to be precise) knew the songs by heart. At one stage, Anna, the younger sister in *Frozen*, is overwhelmed by uncertainty, fear and loss of direction. She sings: 'The life I knew is over, the lights are out/Hello darkness, I'm ready to succumb … You are lost, hope is gone/But you must go on/And do the next right thing…Just do the next right thing/ Take a step, step again/ It is all that I can to do/ The next right thing/ I won't look too far ahead/It's too much for me to take'.

To fall forward (Massumi 2002a), step-by-step, by actively playing with the constraints confronting us – that is how we wrote this book. By surrendering to uncertainty, unpredictability and the unknown, one step at a time.

8.4 Conclusion

We started writing this book during a campus shutdown and are writing this conclusion during a national shutdown. The world around us has changed significantly in the last five years and so have we. Nothing is fixed in this space, not even statues. Especially not statues. Defining educator subjectivity is not what we set out to do. We wanted to see how it forms, what it does, how it changes and what this processual dynamism makes possible. The personal and professional lives of educators are intertwined. In 2020, we saw how the spatial division between workplace and living space was erased due to work from home directives. The collapse of binaries, categories and classification leaves room for difference-in-itself to emerge. When the statue is gone, there is more room to play.

We do not offer a linear narrative of transformation with a happy ending or any kind of ending. We have learned that the process is never complete, always ongoing and not smooth. In our context we have seen rapid and significant change. We have seen how student protest movements made free higher education possible. We have also seen how the ongoing massification of higher education and the commodification of knowledge counters many of the ideals of decolonization. As statues were toppled and the names of campus building changed, there have been changes in the physical spaces of learning. But we are not statues – we are fluid and always in flux. The emergence of educator subjectivity is a responsive and creative engagement with transformation. Transformation as becoming helps us to think of change as continuous energy that shapes subjectivity.

In order to explore the professional/personal continuum, we wanted to see how arts-based research and Deleuzoguattarian concepts, such as the assemblage and the wound-event, could be useful to explore educator subjectivity during social change. Through the process of creating a research assemblage, we encountered subjectivity as an unfolding event. In the context of rapid social change in education this theory and method conflation helps us explore the event of becoming from different temporal perspectives. This theory and method continuum enables us to pay attention, to pause and look back, to look forward, to revisit the wound and to stay with our predicament a little longer.

Liezl says our book should read like a choose-your-own-adventure novel, a wormhole or a rhizome, making surprising connections. Frans says that the formation of subjectivity should be less of a journey and more of an adventure. Marguerite says we are not statues. Our movement in and through and with space and time forms fluid assemblages that are unfrozen. To stay with the trouble and to stay with the predicament mean embracing becoming with the world, becoming-together-with-uncertainty. In order to explore the professional/personal continuum, we wanted to see how arts-based research and Deleuzoguattarian concepts such as the assemblage and the wound-event could be useful to explore educator subjectivity during social change. Through the process of creating a research assemblage, we encountered subjectivity as an unfolding event.

Epilogue

Our journey of writing this book together started at many different points and went in many different directions. Think of this epilogue as the photo negative of the end product of this book. Writing together was a process of living and learning and becoming together. In writing together, we became conscious of the proliferation of knowledge and insights that writing as a multiplicity made possible and produced. We became conscious of how the collaborative process shaped so much of our thinking. In this final section, we offer a glimpse into the 'behind the scenes' of more or less one year of writing together.

23 July 2020: The Last Book Meeting between Marguerite and Liezl

We arrange to meet at the garden centre. It is a tranquil space where we can have a cup of tea while sitting outside in the winter sun. The primroses, cyclamens and pansies are in full bloom, a colourful winter garden that gives some relief in the dreary winter landscape. COVID-19 infections are surging all around South Africa and even meeting face-to-face seems risky at present. We hadn't met in 120 days. The last time we had met, wearing a mask had not been compulsory; in fact, it would have seemed absurd. Now it is the new normal; 120 days ago COVID-19 had seemed a distant threat, on a different continent, but now it is real. We both know people who have tested positive. We have heard of so many people who have died.

So, now we need to write the ending. Now we finish Book. But it is not the end of our story. Despite the global pandemic and everything that has happened,

Figure 31 Drinking tea during a pandemic, 2019.
Photograph, Marguerite Müller.

life goes on. When one route closes, it seems that life finds a different path. Liezl is moving. After today we won't live in the same city anymore.

One Year Earlier: Marguerite

Liezl goes to England. She brings back a blank journal with Van Gogh's painting of The Night Café on the cover. I use it to make notes as I read her copy of Deleuze and Coleman and Ringrose's *Research Methodologies*.

November 2019: WhatsApp Conversation between Liezl and Marguerite

> **Liezl:** Things were a little tense at our collaboration this morning ☺ But I think we have all we need?

Marguerite: I think our different ways of doing things have always had good results … even if it not always smooth sailing to get to the results.

Liezl: You are right. We must remember to send in our abstract in for the conference in May 2020.

December 2020: WhatsApp Conversation between Marguerite and Liezl at a Conference They Both Attended

Liezl: How was your workshop? Mine was ok. Just really a repetition of what autobiographical writing is.

Marguerite: Mine was really interesting. We used Drama and Art to create a new concept. I created rooticles and findicles. I will tell you more about it when we see each other. Are you taking a few days off? I am having trouble to concentrate on work.

Liezl: I see our abstract got accepted. Going to wait a week or two before I work on book again. Need a break.

January 2020: Tense Meeting in Marguerite's Office

These is tension in the air. We are struggling to work together. We feel unsure of what we are doing here. We need to negotiate the writing process. The conflict helps us to define our different roles. We resolve this by writing together.

What are our different roles here? How do we write from such different angles?

Our different perspectives will merge. In the beginning, we explain our different angles and perspectives, and demonstrate it by drawing it.

Marguerite likes to do things and see how they develop, and Liezl likes to know beforehand where this is going. Eventually, we need to accept our different approaches to writing and see what they can make possible. As the book develops, we will become other, become-together – I will incorporate your perspective more and vice versa. This will be a performative element and demonstration of what writing together and becoming together entails. There is a productive tension between our ways of working. Marguerite wants to let it unfold – just to wait and see what happens; let us try it out and then it will show itself, while Liezl needs to plot it out, know the way and see where this is going. Marguerite always overestimates what can be done and sets impossible deadlines. Liezl is more conservative and realistic and considers what we will actually get done. Somehow it worked. We met each other somewhere in the middle.

February 2020: Conversation between Marguerite and Liezl Over Coffee

> **Marguerite:** I feel like we have so many words, words, words. I feel like taking a broom and sweeping the words out the door – clean up a bit – so that I can think.
> **Liezl:** I feel discouraged. The system is broken. How are we helping the students? They come to university and then…
> **Marguerite:** I know. All our words won't matter. From each 100 students who start in Grade 1, only four will complete a university degree. Four out of 100! I feel like just playing with clay. All this writing. I need to get funding for the May conference. Have you applied for the visa yet? It took me a whole day!

20 February 2020: Liezl quoting Barad

Friends, colleagues, students, family members, multiple academic institutions, departments, disciplines, the forest, streams and beaches of the eastern and western coasts, the awesome peace and clarity of early morning hours, and much more were a part of what helped to constitute both this 'book' and its 'author' (2007, x).

March 2020

11 March 2020

> **Liezl:** I am supposed to be writing Chapter 5, but I am stuck. This is probably what writer's block feels like. Something I noticed is that I go into reflection mode fairly quickly, like I was trained in the humanities. Reflect, analyse, interpret, relate, discuss. This is not inherently a bad mode of operation, but it is tricky to move beyond these habits of inhibition, towards a more creative mode. And this made me think of a discussion we had in our reading group the other day. We are reading Wendy Brown's *In the Ruins of Neoliberalism – The Rise of Antidemocratic Politics in the West*. We had only read the introduction, so she will probably address these concerns later in the book, but during the conversation, it became very clear that all of us in the room who are academics are questioning the role of academics and the academy – and theory – in the face of the practical challenges posed by the rise of

Figure 32 Corona virus is here, 2019.
Photograph, Marguerite Müller.

hatred and intolerance. However, the challenges posed by neoliberalism and the conflation of the market and traditional morality and the concomitant rise of the far-right has left the left, well, paralysed, it seems. Brown wants to dismantle the logic of the far-right; she insists on understanding what we are up against instead of merely being reactive and sarcastic (Brown 2019). And this is a good way to proceed, isn't it? You have to have a grip on the thing that you want to change. 'But what if we are complicit in the creation of the monster?' one of my colleagues asked. Should we then destroy ourselves too? We are, after all, part of this society that needs to be dismantled. We also contemplated whether Brown's book is written for the Global North and if it has applicability in our differently complex Global South context.

Anyway, the point that I want to make is that my struggle to write creatively (and not only reflectively or analytically) made me feel as if I was at the door of a new dimension of writing that I have to open. I now have to conflate theory and practice. It's daunting because it's new and I am out of my comfort zone. But it also allows for a more uninhibited mode of engaging with text, Deleuzoguattarian theory and the interviews. My writing struggle and the reading group discussion reminded me of what Deleuze said about the theory/praxis dichotomy (2004a, 206): For theory to develop, it must hit a wall, while practice is then needed to break through the wall. Am I hitting a wall and will my creative conflation of theory and practice help me to break through this wall? The only way to find out is to continue experimentally and with nerves of steel. Stengers (2002, 52) wrote that the problem with theorists is that they refer to their theories as constructs, but that they don't have the skill to operationalize their constructions. This is something that we experienced in our reading group the other day. And it worries me. Because what is the point of writing if we can't apply our own theories to a world so desperately in need of practical solutions?

Deleuze (in conversation with Foucault):

If little children managed to make their protests heard in nursery school, or even simply their questions, it would be enough to derail the whole educational system. In reality, the system in which we live *cannot tolerate anything*: whence you see its radical fragility at every point, and at the same time, it's global repression. In my opinion, you were the first to teach us a fundamental lesson, both in your books and in the practical domain: the indignity of speaking for others. What I mean is we laughed at representation, saying it was over, but we didn't follow this 'theoretical' conversion through – namely theory demanded that those involved finally have their say from a practical standpoint. (Deleuze 2004a, 208)

Liezl: So, I guess I don't have a choice; I have to break through this wall and demolish the writer's block. And my sense is that it can only happen if I allow playfulness to impregnate my habitual analytical writing style. Let the games begin!

19 March 2020

Marguerite: I am trying to work on Chapter 6, but I'm struggling to concentrate. It seems that COVID-19 has taken over our whole lives and our thoughts. Since the president announced a state of emergency, everything seems to have spun out of control and this is now the new normal. The campus has become a ghost town, except for a few last, stranded students and tired-looking staff members. I am trying to get the students to move out of residence, but they are reluctant: What if we get the virus on the bus going home? What if we get it when we are home? It is safer here. Anyway, we don't have money to go home.

My kids are home from school, which makes working extra hard. My husband and I take turns to go to the office, but even there the distractions are too much. What will happen next? We really don't know. I keep thinking of my daughter's fourth birthday coming up and that it will be impossible to invite friends to celebrate. She has been looking forward to this almost all her life and now… I want to make things different for my kids, but right now I feel completely powerless in the face of this tsunami of unpredictability.

I get this email from a student:

Ma'am, I use the computer labs for my work since I don't have a laptop. I thought I'd be able to borrow a friend's laptop, but everyone has been busy working on their assignments that they haven't had a chance to borrow me to do mine. *I thought I had this under control but I don't*, that is why I'm only emailing you now. I am leaving for home tomorrow morning so I have today only to submit. I can use my mom's laptop at home and buy data to submit; however, I will arrive at home on Saturday, which will be too late for submission. Do you perhaps have a suggestion what I can do at this moment?

I thought I had this under control, but I don't. I phone my mom. She asks if I think it is a good idea to keep extra cash in the home in case the banks run out. All of this is getting too much. And then the constant interruptions as I try to focus Chapter 6: the WhatsApp messages, the emails, the news, the noise outside, my colleague speaking too loudly on the phone in the office nearby, my pounding heart!

Lockdown Day 4

It is Monday
We try to start a normal workweek – from home
I sit in behind the computer
I try to focus
The news and the WhatsApp messages keep distracting me

We get used to the silence
The birds return
The mongoose
The field mice…

Lockdown extended by 2 weeks

We fall into a routine

I phone my grandmother's sister
She will be 101 in May
She tells me stories about my grandmother
A bracelet I inherited suddenly has so much more meaning
I miss my grandmother so much

Even though she has been gone so long

The campus is so quiet
Accept for the *kiewiet* birds
Who chase me out of their territory
And the hadida birds
The guinea fowl
The meerkat
even a little deer
animals now roam where humans once ruled

My four-year-old misses her school.
Why, why, why she asks
Why can't we go outside?
Why can't I see my friends?
It is nice to spend so much time with her.
She keeps us busy. She doesn't allow any work to happen on her watch.

8 April 2020

Liezl: Day 13 of the (first) national 21-day lockdown. Yesterday was a difficult day. Who would have thought that a 21-day Deepak Chopra abundance meditation course would have become a lifeline? My prejudices and judgements are failing, one after the other. It's a global pandemic; do whatever works. 'Trying to fix my mind, still trying to fix my mind, trying to work it out' sings Damian Jurado on YouTube. The meditations are helping to calm the obsessive thinking (one really has to question the value of a philosophical training during a time like this!) and uncertainty. And the uncertainty is rife. I realized that in order to go 'forward', to function every day, I will have to be willing to do a double back somersault with three twists into the unknown. I will have to work with what I can work with, try to work my way into the unknown with what is known to me. No attachment to outcomes, no expectations. Where will I be in a year's time? Who knows? Do I currently have a job? Yes. What is expected of me in this job? To research and write. Well, there's my plan. At least I still have a job! If I start worrying now about my life in a year's time, I might get so depressed and I won't get any work done, which might inevitably lead to me living on the streets… Hence, the plan of action is a double back-somersault into the unknown. We will need loads of inner strength to get through this. That, and our health, of course. Focus. Breathe in, breathe out.

I have to work on Chapter 5 of our book, but I'm really struggling. It's about the wound as an event. Quite relevant in these times; if we consider COVID-19 as an event, when did it start? And what will be the consequences of all of this? And how can we be worthy of what happens to us?

I also wonder when I will be able to go home. I am stuck in another province and staying with my sister and her family. Section 21 of the Bill of Rights of South Africa refers to Freedom of Movement and Residence:

21. Freedom of movement and residence
1. Everyone has the right to freedom of movement.
2. Everyone has the right to leave the Republic.
3. Every citizen has the right to enter, to remain in and to reside anywhere in the Republic.
4. Every citizen has the right to a passport.[1]

This right, among others, has been suspended for the period of the lockdown. How we took these freedoms for granted!

30 April 2020

Liezl: The emotional turmoil continues. Who *are* we (becoming)?

1 May 2020

Liezl: Just arrived back home from my first jog in the neighbourhood's streets in 35 days. We moved from level 5 lockdown to level 4 today, which allows us to go for a run or walk in the mornings between 6am

Figure 33 Force Majeure, 2020.
Screenshot of TextChat.

and 9am. A feeling of elation overwhelmed me and I never thought a run in the streets could be such an emotional experience! In the street, the usually reserved residents smiled friendly at each other, people in cars were waving at those walking. Strange! But wonderful. Now all of us know what it feels like when your freedom is taken away from you. Never, never, never again.

May 2020

Liezl: Sjoe! What a day. What a week. I nearly lost my mind yesterday. This Deleuze/event work is fucking hardcore and is hard on the brain, especially during a global pandemic.

5 May 2020

Liezl: The ordering principles of everything we know is shifting. It's in the air, one can feel it. What we perceived of as important, or those principles that guided actions and future driven endeavours, are changing, and we don't know yet what it's changing into.

12 May 2020

Marguerite: I made a painting of an African violet. My grandmother used to keep these in her kitchen window. I have tried to do the same but mine dies every time. So now I made a painting of African violets… are they really African?

19 May 2020: Email from Liezl to Marguerite

I am reading *Alice in Wonderland*, again. This first paragraph had me thinking of you! 'Alice was beginning to get very tired of sitting by her sister on the bank, and of having nothing to do: once or twice she had peeped into the book her sister was reading, but it had no pictures or conversations in it, 'and what is the use of a book,' thought Alice, 'without pictures or conversations?' (Carrol 2012, 5).

20 May 2020: Liezl Reading *Alice in Wonderland*

Alice thought she might as well wait, as she had nothing else to do, and perhaps after all it might tell her something worth hearing. For some minutes it puffed away without speaking, but at last it unfolded its arms, took the hookah out of its mouth again, and said, 'So you think you're changed, do you?'

'I'm afraid I am, sir,' said Alice; 'I can't remember things as I used – and I don't keep the same size for ten minutes together!' (Carrol 2012, 51–3).

June 2020

And when the journey ends one day,
when I become one with everything
Perhaps someone will pick me up
underneath a lemon tree

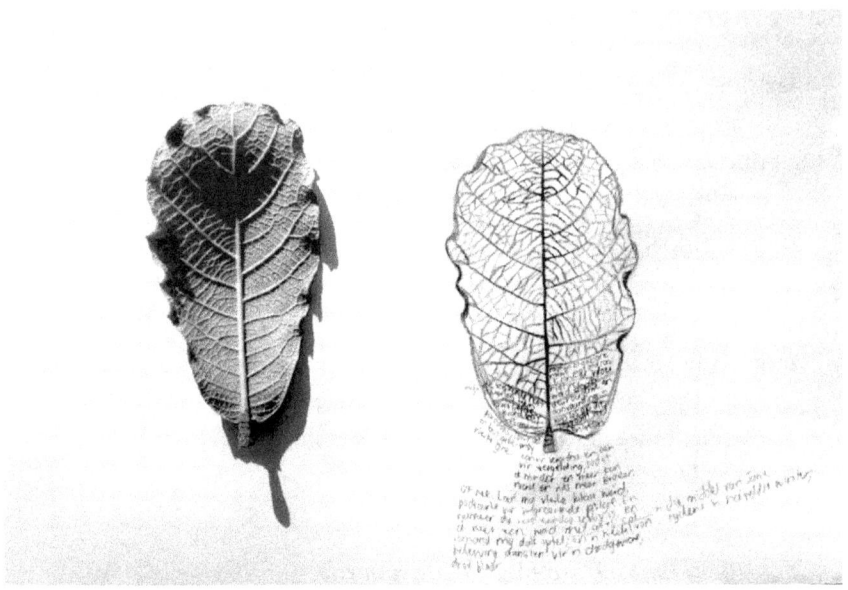

Figure 34 And when the journey ends, 2020. *Drawing, Liezl Dick.*

    and in the middle of a highveld winter
    a universe of experiences
    will be masquerading as just another dry
    dead leaf.

12 June 2020: Marguerite's Children's Experiences of Lockdown

'It is like a little piece of sadness that is inside of my heart … and it is always there … it never goes away'. This is how Josh describes the third month of lockdown, and being away from grandparents and friends and family.

'Maybe we are in a movie … because everyone else is on the other side of the screen … and we cannot hug or kiss them'. This is how Mei understands our new reality.

13 June 2020: TextChat message from Liezl to Marguerite

Thank you for the chapter, I love it! It inspires me too keep on writing. I just spoke to an actor friend of mine in Cape Town who wanted to bounce off ideas and the conversation made me realize: The counter-actualization we are writing about in the wound-chapter – this is what happens when the participants tell their stories. Fullstop. The interpretation of the story is *not* the crux; the crux is the story itself and the fact that is has been shared. I don't have to solve the problems of the educators and I don't have to answer their questions. We just have to tell their stories. The narrative is all we have. Now is not the time for final conclusions. And this is exactly why I think the notion of the rhizome works so well for our book.

1 July 2020

Happy 40th, Liezl.

11 July 2020

Marguerite: As I review our work, I am reminded of one of my favourite academic articles: 'Blue Collar Qualitative Research: A Rant' by Johnny Saldaña (2014). Let me recap some of my favourite parts here:

'If all there is these days is ambiguity, uncertainty, unresolved complexity, and unanswered questions, then Jesus Christ, what's it all for? Let's just pack up and go home' (Saldaña 2014, 978).

'There's some misguided people out there who think that alls they gotta do is come up with a smart question and their job's done. Well, fuck that noise. I want answers. I need answers. Some folks will say, "Well, it's not that simple," to which I usually reply, "It's prob'ly not that complicated, either." Straight talk – *sometimes the most profound thoughts are said usin' the simplest of words*' (Saldaña 2014, 978; emphasis added).

'Stop wastin' paper or conference time or digital space if you don't have any answers yourself to the questions you ask. Do your god-damn job as a researcher and *answer the goddamn questions you pose*' (Saldaña 2014, 979; emphasis in original).

'*Remember that the original meanin' of datum is 'somethin' given.' Data is a gift, so be thankful for it when it's given to you and treat it with respect*' (Saldaña 2014, 978; emphasis added).

'If you feel you *gotta* cite Foucault, Derrida, Deleuze, or Habermas in any of your work, you need to bring it down a notch' (Saldaña 2014, 978).

If you use any combination of the *words body, bod-ies, bodied, bodying, embodied, embodying,* or *embodiment* more than five times in one paragraph, you need to bring it down a notch' (Saldaña 2014, 978).

August 2020

Marguerite (inspired by Saldaña (2014)): I write a middle-class sick-and-tired academic rant:

Now I am sick and tired of the calls for COVID-19 special issues, the articles to fill the sudden paucity – the gap in COVID 19 research. Sick and tired. Fuck the gap.
If I have to answer *one* more survey about the challenges I am experiencing, I am going to lose it!
What are your challenges with the new online mode of lecturing?
What are your challenges as a female academic?
My challenge is avoiding all these surveys.
I am not a blue collar researcher. I am trapped in middle-class academic mediocrity.
COVID-19 is not a gap to be filled with our obsession with publications, this is happening to us. It is as if the image of death with its great scythe walking among us has come alive. Every day on the staff group we see: condolences to … with the passing of … I am angered by exploitative and opportunistic academic research that cannot take a minute to breathe and think about what is happening before it becomes *another* special issue, *another* conference, *another* publication. I know we need to engage with it, to make sense of it, have to write about it. But what have we become when our only response to the world is to ask, How can I publish this? What can I get out of it? What can I extort from this? What is the difference between encounter and extraction? What do we add as researchers? What do we give? What do we take? 'Colonisation is going on when the world we inhabit is understood as a vast field of data awaiting extraction' (Mbembe 2019).

August 2020: Email from Liezl to Marguerite: Nick Cave's Blog, The Red Hand Files[2]

Our task is both simple and extremely difficult. Our task is to remain patient and vigilant and to not lose heart — for we are the destination. We are the portals from which the idea explodes, forced forth by its yearning to arrive. We are the revelators, the living instruments through which the idea announces itself — the flourishing and the blooming — but we are also the waiting and the wondering and the worrying.

August 2020: From Frans to Marguerite

SOMETIMES
by David Whyte[3]
Sometimes
if you move carefully
through the forest,
breathing
like the ones
in the old stories,
who could cross
a shimmering bed of leaves
without a sound,
you come to a place
whose only task
is to trouble you
with tiny
but frightening requests,
conceived out of nowhere
but in this place
beginning to lead everywhere.
Requests to stop what
you are doing right now,
and
to stop what you
are becoming
while you do it,
questions
that can make
or unmake
a life,
questions
that have patiently
waited for you,
questions
that have no right
to go away.

(our emphasis)

29 August 2020: How Do We End This?

Marguerite: It is hard to concentrate… the sound of the construction vehicle… emails from students.
Liezl: I need another cup of tea. I am so tired.
Marguerite: We are almost done.
Liezl: I wish we had a huge budget so we could personify Becoming and Uncertainty into cartoon characters.
Marguerite: I would like to jump on Uncertainty.
Liezl: This could become a lifelong project.

They laugh.

Figure 35 We laugh, 2020.
Screenshot.

Liezl: I read something interesting about what Rajchman said about Deleuze and experimentation. Listen to this:

He [Deleuze] pushes the experience or experimentalism of thought into a zone before the establishment of a stable, intersubjective 'we', and makes it a matter not of recognizing ourselves or the things in our world, but rather or encounter with what we can't yet 'determine' – to what we can't yet describe or agree upon, since we don't yet even have the words. (Rajchman 2001, 20)

Marguerite: Ok, but I think we need to finish this now. Like you always say: you can never finish a book, you have to abandon it.

Notes

Chapter 2

1 H. Bergson, *Matter and Memory*. Translated by Nancy Margaret Paul and W. Scott Palmer (London: Allen and Unwin, 1911).
2 C. Maartens-Van Vuuren, 'Roots, Rhizomes and Radicles. Reflections on Memories and Voyage of Becoming'. Master's thesis. Bloemfontein: University of the Free State (2019).

Chapter 3

1 In this book we made a conscious decision to use the racial categories inherited from pre-1994 apartheid South Africa, namely white, black, coloured (mixed race) and Asian as they emerged as identity markers in the narratives of participants. In this book we used the terms as used by the participants during conversations. We do not agree with the racial categorization in any form, but we do acknowledge that racial markers are necessary for having meaningful conversations about lived experience in our context. Our context is not 'colour-blind'. Our use of racial markers are, thus, informed by the fact that the lived experiences in South Africans remain determined largely by constructed racial categories, and these categories are still widely used within education institutions. The categories are also enshrined in the memory of a post-apartheid society. Therefore, the acknowledgement of the impact of prevailing racialized identities on the lived experiences of South Africans is important in the education context.

Chapter 4

1 Mixed masala is a term used in South African English to indicate a mixture of things. Masala literally means a mixture of curry spices.
2 https://www.goodreads.com/author/quotes/13275.Charles_Bukowski.

Chapter 5

1. University of the Free State. 2018. 'Public Consultation on MT Steyn Statue Begins with Exhibition'. About the UFS. 8 July 2018. https://www.ufs.ac.za/about-the-ufs/mt-steyn-statue-public-consultation
2. 'From 12 January 1960 to 30 April 1961 C. R. Swart was the ninth and last governor-general of the Union of South Africa. From 31 May 1961 he was the first state president of the Republic of South Africa for six years. He was thus the only person who was governor-general and state president. He was also responsible for certain measures that were a result of the NP's racial policy: the Immorality Act and the acts regulating separate amenities; the banning of the Communist Party of South Africa (CPSA, South African Communist Party (SACP) after 1953) and the restriction of other organizations regarded as subversive. Swart was severely criticized for his share in the banning of Albert Luthuli and other African National Congress (ANC) leaders. *Source*: https://www.sahistory.org.za/people/charles-robberts-blackie-swart.During the 2016 #FeesMustFall protest, protesters toppled the statue an dragged it into a nearby pond. It was removed from the UFS grounds after that incident.

Chapter 6

1. Please see footnote 1 in Chapter 3.
2. Pijoos, Iavan. 2016. 'UFS Students Demand Jansen's Removal | News24'. News24, 25 February 2016. https://www.news24.com/news24/southafrica/news/ufs-students-demand-jansens-removal-20160225.
3. In 1991, South African government schools moved to what was known as a Model C system. These schools were former whites-only schools and followed a semi-private fee paying structure. This meant that parents paid fees to supplement the government subsidy. Most of the former Model C schools are now known as Quintile 5 schools. From 2006, South African schools have been classified into five different quintiles, each in accordance with the relative wealth of the surrounding communities. On a scale of reference, schools in poor communities will be categorized as Quintile 1, whereas schools from rich communities are categorized as Quintile 5. In Quintile 5 schools, the government gives less funding than for Quintile 1, and parents will pay fees to supplement the school funds. Many people still use the term Model C to refer to former white and wealthy schools.
4. J. De Villiers, 'EXPLAINER | Why UFS Quietly Removed a Statue of President MT Steyn'. News24, 30 June 2020. https://www.news24.com/news24/analysis/explainer-why-ufs-quietly-removed-a-statue-of-president-mt-steyn-20200630.

Chapter 7

1 'Stephen (Steve) Bantu Biko was a popular voice of Black liberation in South Africa between the mid-1960s and his death in police detention in 1977. This was the period in which both the ANC and the PAC had been officially banned and the disenfranchised Black population (especially the youth) were highly receptive to the prospect of a new organisation that could carry their grievances against the Apar state. Thus it was that Biko's Black Consciousness Movement (BCM) came to prominence and although Biko was not its only leader, he was its most recognisable figure.' *Source*: https://www.sahistory.org.za/people/stephen-bantu-biko.

2 One of South Africa's most established and experienced artists in the field of public sculpture, Willem Boshoff, was commissioned to produce a major sculpture for the core of the campus. Boshoff is well known for his innovative and his conceptual pieces. He has produced numerous public art pieces nationally and aboard including commissions from the University of Johannesburg, the Constitutional Court, the Mpumalanga Legislature in Nelspruit and South Africa House at Trafalgar Square in London. His work is deeply involved in relationships and social interaction and is generally focussed on bringing about conversation. The sculpture he created for the university is installed in the area between the H. van der Merwe Scholtz Hall and the Main Building. Boshoff's work comprises a 32-ton polished black granite rock that was quarried at Boschpoort Granite in Belfast, Mpumalanga. The rock has engravings that resemble the prehistoric rock engravings (also known as petroglyphs) of Driekopseiland (a prehistoric rock art site situated close to Kimberley). Added to the engravings are sandblasted inscriptions in six languages with verses and quotes that refer to 'rock' and inspire thought and completion. Boshoff has made other works of a similar nature, including Children of the Stars, situated at the Cradle of Humankind.

Epilogue

1. https://www.concourt.org.za/images/phocadownload/the_text/english-2013.pdf
2. N. Cave, 'What Do You Do When the Lyrics Just Aren't Coming?' Blog. The Red Hand Files (blog). August #108 (2020). https://www.theredhandfiles.com/the-lyrics-just-arent-coming/.
3. https://www.davidwhyte.com/poetry-2.

References

Aoki, Ted T. 1993. 'Legitimating a Lived Curriculum: Towards a Curricular Landscape of Multiplicity'. *Journal of Curriculum and Supervision* 8 (3): 255–68.

Aoki, Ted T. 2005. 'Signs of Vitality in Curriculum Scholarship'. In *Curriculum in a New Key: The Collected Works of Ted Aoki*, edited by William F. Pinar and Rita. L. Irwin, 229–34. New York: Hillsdale.

Arendt, Hannah. 1994. 'Understanding and Politics (the Difficulties of Understanding)'. In *Essays in Understanding 1930–1954*, edited by Jerome Kohn, 203–37. New York: Harcourt, Brace.

Barad, Karen. 2003. 'Posthumanist Performativity: Toward an Understanding of How Matter Comes to Matter'. *Signs: Journal of Women in Culture and Society* 28 (3): 801–31.

BBC News. 2020. 'Huge Anti-Racism Protests Held across US', 7 June 2020, sec. US and Canada. https://www.bbc.com/news/world-us-canada-52951093.

Biesta, Gert. 2017. *Letting Art Teach*. Arnhem: ArtEZ Press.

Biesta, Gert. 2020a. 'Rediscovering the Beauty and Risk of Education Research and Teaching: An Interview with Gert Biesta ByStephen Heimans'. *Asia-Pacific Journal of Teacher Education* 48 (2): 101–11. https://doi.org/10.1080/1359866X.2020.1731422.

Biesta, Gert. 2020b. 'Reimagining the New Pedagogical Possibilities for Universities Post-Covid-19'. *Educational Philosophy and Theory*, Issue: Reimagining the New Pedagogical Possibilities for Universities Post-Covid-19, June, 1–44. https://doi.org/10.1080/00131857.2020.1777655.

Boulton-Funke, Adrienne. 2014. 'Narrative Form and Yam Lau's Room: The Encounter in Arts Based Research'. *International Journal of Education & the Arts* 15 (17): 1–16.

Bousquet, Joë. 1979. *Le Meneur de Lune*. Paris: Albin Michel.

Braidotti, Rosi. 2000. *Metamorphosis: Towards a Materialist Theory of Becoming*. Cambridge, MA: Polity Press.

Braidotti, Rosi. 2011a. *Nomadic Subjects: Embodiment and Sexual Difference in Contemporary Feminist Theory*. Cambridge, MA: Polity Press.

Braidotti, Rosi. 2011b. *Nomadic Theory: The Portable Rosi Braidotti*. New York: Columbia University Press. https://doi.org/10.7312/brai15190.

Brown, Wendy. 2019. *In the Ruins of Neoliberalism: the Rise of Antidemocratic Politics in the West*. New York: Columbia University Press.

Burke, Meghan A. 2011. 'Discursive Fault Lines: Reproducing White Habitus in a Racially Diverse Community'. *Critical Sociology* 38 (5): 645–68.

Cahnmann-Taylor, Melisa., and Richard Siegesmund. 2017. *Arts-Based Research in Education: Foundations for Practice*. New York: Routledge.
Carrol, Lewis. 2012. *Alice's Adventures in Wonderland*. London: Vintage Books.
Chase, Susan E. 2011. 'Narrative Inquiry: Still a Field in the Making'. In *The Sage Handbook of Qualitative Research*, edited by Norman K. Denzin and Yvonna. S. Lincoln, 421–34. Thousand Oaks, CA: Sage.
Cixous, Hélène, and Mireille Calle-Gruber. 1997. *Hélène Cixous, Rootprints: Memory and Life Writing*. London: Psychology Press.
Clandinin, D. Jean., and F. Michael Connelly. 2000. *Narrative Inquiry: Experience and Story in Qualitative Research*. San Francisco, CA: Jossey-Bass.
Coleman, Rebecca, and Jessica Ringrose. 2014. 'Introduction'. In *Deleuze and Research Methodologies*, edited by Rebecca Coleman and Jessica Ringrose, 1–22. Edinburgh: Edinburgh University Press.
Colman, Felicity J. 2010. 'Affect'. In *The Deleuze Dictionary*, edited by Adrian Parr, Revised, 11–13. Edinburgh: Edinburgh University Press.
Crow, Nosy, and Sebastien Braun. 2016. *Big Bug Log. A Bugsy Bug Adventure*. London: Nosy Crow.
Davies, Bronwyn, Jenny Browne, Susanne Gannon, Eileen Honan, and Margaret Somerville. 2005. 'Embodied Women at Work in Neoliberal Times and Places'. *Gender, Work & Organization* 12 (4): 343–62.
Davies, Bronwyn, and Susanne Gannon. 2012. 'Collective Biography and the Entangled Enlivening of Being'. *International Review of Qualitative Research* 5(4): 357–76.
Deleuze, Gilles. 1990. *The Logic of Sense*. New York: Columbia University Press.
Deleuze, Gilles. 2004a. *Desert Islands and Other Texts 1953–1974*. Edited by David Lapoujade. New York: Semiotext(e).
Deleuze, Gilles. 2004b. *Difference and Repetition*. London: Continuum.
Deleuze, Gilles, and Félix, Guattari. 2008. *A Thousand Plateaus – Capitalism and Schizophrenia*. London: Continuum.
Denzin, Norman K. 2013. 'The Death of Data?' *Cultural Studies ↔ Critical Methdologies* 13 (4): 353–6.
Dick, Liezl. 2016. 'The Integration of Racialized Subjectivities at a Higher Education Undergraduate Female Residence: A Deleuzoguattarian Perspective'. Unpublished PhD thesis, Bloemfontein, South Africa: University of the Free State.
Dick, Liezl, Frans Kruger, Marguerite Müller, and Angelo Mockie. 2019. 'Transformative Pedagogy as Academic Performance: #ShimlaPark as a Plane of Immanence'. *Cultural Studies ↔ Critical Methodologies* 19 (2): 84–90.
Eisner, Elliot W. 1990. 'Creative Curriculum Development and Practice'. *Journal of Curriculum and Supervision* 6 (1): 62–73.
Eisner, Elliot W. 2008. 'Persistent Tensions in Arts-Based Research'. In *Arts-Based Research in Education. Foundations for Practice*, edited by Melisa Cahnmann-Taylor and Richard Siegesmund, 17–27. New York: Routledge.

Eliastam, John, Julian Muller, Marguerite Müller, and Sheila Trahar. 2019. 'Fictionalisation and Research'. In *Unfolding Narratives of Ubuntu in Southern Africa*, edited by Julian Muller, John Eliastam and Sheila Trahar, 12–28. New York: Routledge.

Erasmus, Zimitri. 2017. *Race Otherwise*. Johannesburg: Wits University Press.

Fanon, Frantz. 2007. *Black Skin, White Masks*. New York: Grove Press.

Finley, Susan. 2012. 'Art-Based Research'. In *Handbook of the Arts in Qualitative Research: Perspectives, Methodologies, Examples and Issues*, edited by J. Gary Knowles and Ardra L. Cole, 71–82. Thousand Oaks, CA: Sage.

Finley, Susan. 2017. 'Critical Arts-Based Inquiry: Performances of Resistance Politics'. In *The Sage Handbook of Qualitative Research*, edited by N. K. Denzin and Yvonne S. Lincoln, 561–75. Thousand Oaks, CA: Sage.

Freire, Paolo. 2003. *Pedagogy of the Oppressed*. New York: Continuum.

Gaiman, Neil. 2018. *Art Matters. Because Your Imagination Can Change the World*. London: Headline.

Gale, Ken. 2020. 'The Anthropocene, Affect, and Autoethnography?' *Journal of Autoethnography* 1 (3): 304–8. https://doi.org/10.1525/joae.2020.1.3.304.

Gannon, Susanne, and Marnina Gonick. 2019. 'Collective Biography as a Feminist Methodology'. In *Strategies for Resisting Sexism in the Academy. Higher Education, Gender and Intersectionality*, edited by Gail Crimmins, 2017–224. Cham: Palgrave Macmillan.

Grosz, Elizabeth. 1999. 'Thinking the New: Of Futures yet Unthought'. In *Becomings: Explorations in Time, Memory, and Futures*, edited by Elizabeth Grosz. London: Cornell University Press.

Guattari, Félix. 2015. *Psychoanalysis and Transversality: Texts and Interviews, 1955–1971*. South Pasadena: Semiotext(e).

Haraway, Donna J. 2016. *Staying with the Trouble: Making Kin in the Chthulucene*. Durham, NC: Duke University Press.

Hickey-Moody, Anna. 2014. 'Affect as Method: Feelings, Aesthetics and Affective Pedagogy'. In *Deleuze and Research Methodologies*, edited by Jessica Ringrose and Rebecca Coleman, 79–95. Edinburgh: Edinburgh University Press.

Hickey-Moody, Anna. 2017. 'Arts Practice as Method, Urban Spaces and Intra-Active Faiths'. *International Journal of Inclusive Education* 21 (11): 1083–96. https://doi.org/10.1080/13603116.2017.1350317.

Honan, Eileen, and David Bright. 2016. 'Writing a Thesis Differently'. *International Journal of Qualitative Studies in Education* 29 (5): 731–43. https://doi.org/10.1080/09518398.2016.1145280.

hooks, bell. 2003. *Teaching Community. A Pedagogy of Hope*. New York: Routledge.

Ingold, T. 2010. 'Drawing Together. Materials Gestures, Lines'. In *Experiments in Holism: Theory and Practice in Contemporary Anthropology*, edited by Ton Otto and Nils Buband, 299–313. Oxford: Blackwell.

Jama, Mpho. 2017. 'Applying a Humanistic Pedagogy to Advance and Integrate Humane Values in a Medical School Environment'. *Perspectives in Education* 35 (1): 28–39.

Jansen, Jonathan. J. 2017a. 'Introduction – Part II. Decolonising the University Curriculum given a Dysfunctional School System?' *Journal of Education* 68: 4–13.

Jansen, Jonathan. J. 2017b. 'Sense and Nonsense in the Decolonisation of Curriculum'. In *As by Fire. The End of the South African University*, edited by Jonathan J. Jansen, 153–71. Cape Town: Tafelberg.

Janz, Bruce. 2019. 'Scholarly Cognition, Place and the Event'. In *Philosophy on the Border: Decoloniality and the Shudder of Origin*, edited by Leonhard Praeg, 54–70. Pietermaritzburg: University of KwaZulu-Natal Press.

Johansson, Lotta. 2016. 'Post-Qualitative Line of Flight and the Confabulative Conversation: A Methodological Ethnography, International'. *Journal of Qualitative Studies in Education* 29 (4): 445–66. https://eric.ed.gov/?id=EJ1091071.

Keet, André. 2014. 'Epistemic "othering" and the Decolonisation of Knowledge'. *Africa Insight* 44 (1): 23–37.

Keet, André, Sahar. D. Sattarzadeh, and Anne. Munene. 2017. 'An Awkward, Uneasy (de)Coloniality Higher Education and Knowledge Otherwise'. *Education as Change* 21 (1): 1–12. http://dx.doi.org/10.17159/1947-9417/2017/2741.

Koro-Ljungberg, Mirka, and Justin Hendricks. 2018. 'Narratives and Nested-Time'. *Qualitative Inquiry*, August, 1–10. https://doi.org/10.1177/1077800418792021.

Kruger, Frans. 2020. 'The Movement of Thought: Mapping Knowledge-Growing'. In *Scholarly Engagement and Decolonisation – Views from South Africa, the Netherlands and the United States*, edited by Maurice Crul, Halleh Ghorashi and Abel Valenzuela Jr, 1:323–42. On Education Transformation. Stellenbosch: Sun Media.

Lawlor, Leonard. 2019. 'The Ultimate Meaning of Counter-Actualization: On the Ethics of the Univocity of Being in Deleuze's Logic of Sense. Plenary'. In Lecturer series at Academic Camp: 12th Annual Deleuze and Guattari Academic Camp, Royal Holloway University of London. 1–5 July 2019. Royal Holloway University of London, London.

Lazenby, Jacobus A. A., and Keletso Radebe. 2011. 'Students' Perceptions about Institutional Transformation at the University of the Free State'. *African Journal of Business Management* 5 (14): 5766–74.

Le Grange, Lesley. 2010. 'South African Curriculum Studies: A Historical Perspective and Autobiographical Account'. In *Curriculum Studies in South Africa: Intellectual Histories and Present Circumstances*, edited by William Pinar, 177–200. Basingstoke: Palgrave Macmillan.

Le Grange, Lesley. 2018. 'Decolonising, Africanising, Indigenising, and Internationalising: Opportunities to (Re)Imagine the Field'. *Journal of Education* 74: 4–18.

Lingis, Alphonso. 2002. 'Murmurs of Life. An Interview'. In *Hope: New Philosophies for Change*, edited by Mary Zournazi, 22–42. London: Routledge.

Loots, Gerrit, Kathleen. Coppens and Jasmina. Sermijn. 2017. 'Practising a Rhizomatic Perspective'. In *Doing Narrative Research*, edited by Molly Andrews, Corinne Squire, and Maria Tamboukou, 108–25. Thousand Oaks, CA: Sage.

Manning, Erin. 2015. 'Artfulness'. In *The Nonhuman Turn*, edited by Richard Grusin, 49–79. Minneapolis: University of Minnesota Press.
Manning, Erin. 2016. *The Minor Gesture*. Durham, NC: Duke University Press.
Marais, Willemien, and Johann C. De Wet. 2009. 'The Reitz Video: Inviting Outrage and/or Pity?' *Communitas* 14 (1): 27–42.
Masny, Diana. 2013. *Cartographies of Becoming in Education: A Deleuze-Guattari Perspective*. Rotterdam: Sense Publishers. https://www.tandfonline.com/doi/abs/10.1080/02601370.2014.946243?journalCode=tled20.
Massey, Doreen. 2005. *For Space*. Los Angeles, CA: Sage.
Massumi, Brian. 2002a. 'Navigating Movements. An Interview'. In *Hope: New Philosophies for Change*, edited by Mary Zournazi, 210–42. New York: Psychology Press.
Massumi, Brian. 2002b. *Parables for the Virtual: Movement, Affect, Sensation*. Durham, NC: Duke University Press.
Mazzei, Lisa. A. 2014. 'Desire Undone: Productions of Privilege, Power and Voice'. In *Deleuze and Research Methodologies*, edited by Rebecca Coleman and Jessica Ringrose, 96–108. Edinburgh: Edinburgh University Press.
Mbembe, Achille Joseph. 2016. 'Decolonizing the University: New Directions'. *Arts and Humanities in Higher Education* 15 (1): 29–45.
Mbembe, Achille Joseph. 2019. Thoughts on the Planetary: An interview with Achille Mbembe. Interview by Sindre Bangstad and Nilsen Tumyr Torbjørn. New Frame. https://www.newframe.com/thoughts-on-the-planetary-an-interview-with-achille-mbembe/.
McAdams, Dan., and Kate C. McLean. 2013. 'Narrative Identity'. *Current Directions in Psychological Science* 22 (3): 233–38.
McKay, Loraine, and Viviana Sappa. 2019. 'Harnessing Creativity through Arts-Based Research to Support Teachers' Identity Development'. *Journal of Adult and Continuing Education*. https://doi.org/10.1177/1477971419841068.
McNiff, Shaun. 2008. 'Art-Based Research'. In *Handbook of the Arts in Qualitative Research: Perspectives, Methodologies, Examples and Issues*, edited by J. Gary Knowles and Ardra L. Cole, 29–40. Thousand Oaks, CA: Sage.
Müller, Marguerite. 2016. 'A Collaborative Self-Study of Educators Working towards Anti-Oppressive Practice in Higher Education'. Unpublished PhD thesis, Bloemfontein, South Africa: University of the Free State.
Müller, Marguerite. 2017. 'Are You Happy Now? A Fictional Narrative Exploration of Educator Experiences in Higher Education during the Time of #FeesMustFall'. *Education as Change* 21 (2): 2017.
Müller, Marguerite. 2018. 'A Critical Arts-Based Narrative of Five Educators Working in Higher Education During an Era of Transformation in South Africa'. *Journal of Education* 72: 89–104. https://doi.org/10.17159/2520-9868/i72a06.
Müller, Marguerite. 2020. 'Having Fun Seriously Matters: A Visual Arts-Based Narrative of Methodological Inventiveness'. *Journal of Education (SAERA)* 78: 43–57.

Müller, Marguerite, and Liezl Dick. 2019. 'Shooting for the Moon: The Journey to Professionalising Student Affairs'. Colloquium, UFS campus, Bloemfontein, South Africa.

Müller, Marguerite, and Adré Le Roux and Frans Kruger. 2021. 'Diffractive Memory-Stories and Response-Activeness in Teaching Social Justice'. *Discourse: Studies in the Cultural Politics of Education*. https://doi.org/10.1080/01596306.2021.1902944.

Nietzsche, Friedrich. 1968. *The Will to Power*. New York: Vintage Books.

Patton, Paul. 1997. 'The World Seen From Within: Deleuze and the Philosophy of Events'. *Theory & Event* 1 (1). https://doi.org/0.1353/tae.1991.0006.

Patton, Paul. 2006. 'The Event of Colonization'. In *Deleuze and the Contemporary World*, 108–24. Deleuze Connections. Edinburgh: Edinburgh University Press. https://www.jstor.org/stable/10.3366/j.ctt1r245n.

Petersen, Francis. 2019. 'University of the Free State's Position on Gender-Based Violence'. *News ArchiveUFS*. https://www.ufs.ac.za/templates/news-archive/campus-news/2019/september/university-of-the-free-state-s-position-on-gender-based-violence.

Pinar, William F. 2012. *What Is Curriculum Theory?* London: Routledge.

Pithouse-Morgan, Kathleen, S'phiwe Madondo, and EdwinaGrossi. 2019. 'The Promise of Poetry Belongs to Us All: Poetic Professional Learning in Teacher-Researchers' Memory-Work'. In *Memory Mosaics: Researching Teacher Professional Learning Through Artful Memory-Work*, edited by Kathleen Pithouse-Morgan, Daisy Pillay and Claudia Mitchell, 133–53. Cham: Springer.

Pullen, Alison, Carl Rhodes and Torkild Thanem. 2017. 'Affective Politics in Gendered Organizations: Affirmative Notes on Becoming-Woman'. *Organization* 24 (1): 105–23.

Rajchman, John. 2001. *The Deleuze Connections*. Cambridge, MA: MIT Press.

Republic of South Africa. 1996. *South African Schools Act, 1996. President's Office No. 1867*. http://www.saflii.org.za/za/legis/num_act/sasa1996228/#:~:text=84%20OF%201996%3A%20SOUTH%20AFRICAN%20SCHOOLS%20ACT%2C%201996.&text=WHEREAS%20it%20is%20necessary%20to,text%20signed%20by%20the%20President.

Reynolds, Jack. 2007. 'Wounds and Scars: Deleuze on the Time and Ethics of the Event'. *Deleuze Studies* 1 (2): 52–74. https://doi.org/10.3366/E1750224108000056.

Rilke, Rainer M. 2011. *Letters to a Young Poet*. London: Penguin UK.

Rosiek, Jerry Lee, and Jimmy Snyder. 2018. 'Narrative Inquiry and New Materialsim: Stories as (Not Necessarily Benign) Agents'. *Qualitative Inquiry*, August, 1–12. https://doi.org/:https://doi.org/10.1177/1077800418784326.

Saldaña, Johnny. 2014. 'Blue Collar Qualitative Research: A Rant'. *Qualitative Inquiry* 20 (8): 976–80.

Schreiber, Birgit, Teboho Moja, and Terry M. Luescher. 2020. 'Racism and Corona: Two Viruses Affecting Higher Education and the Student Experience'. *Journal of Student Affairs in Africa* 8 (1): v–ix.

Semetsky, Inna. 2003. 'The Problematics of Human Subjectivity: Gilles Deleuze and the Deweyan Legacy'. *Studies in Philosophy and Education* 22: v–ix.
Spinoza, Baruch. 1957. *The Ethics of Spinoza*. Secaucus, NJ: Citadel Press.
St. Pierre, Elizabeth Adams. 2011. 'Post Qualitative Research. The Critique and the Coming After'. In *The Sage Handbook of Qualitative Research*, edited by Norman K. Denzin and Yvonna S. Lincoln, 611–25. Thousand Oaks, CA: Sage.
St. Pierre, Elizabeth Adams. 2013. 'Appearance of Data'. *Cultural Studies ↔ Critical Methodologies* 13 (4): 223–7. https://doi.org/10.1177/1077800419863005.
St. Pierre, Elizabeth Adams. 2019. 'Post Qualitative Inquiry, the Refusal of Method, and the Risk of the New'. *Qualitative Inquiry*, July, 1077800419863005. https://doi.org/10.1177/1077800419863005.
Stagoll, Cliff. 2010. 'Event'. In *The Deleuze Dictionary*, edited by Adrian Parr, Rev. edn, 89–91. Edinburgh: Edinburgh University Press.
Stengers, Isabelle. 2002. 'A "Cosmo-Politics" – Risk, Hope, Change. An Interview'. In *Hope: New Philosophies for Change*, edited by Mary Zournazi, 224–73. London: Routledge.
Steyn, Melissa. 2012. 'The Ignorance Contract: Recollections of Apartheid Childhoods and the Construction of Epistemologies of Ignorance'. *Identities* 19 (1): 8–25.
Stubbs, Aelred. 1987. *I Write What I Like: Selected Writings, Steve Biko*. Oxford: Heinemann. https://press.uchicago.edu/ucp/books/book/chicago/I/bo3632310.html.
Sweet, Joseph D, Emppu Nurminen, and Mirka Koro-Ljungberg. 2019. 'Becoming Research with Shadow Work: Combining Artful Inquiry With Research-Creation'. *Qualitative Inquiry* 26 (3–4): 338–99. https://doi.org/10.1177/1077800419857764.
Tamboukou, Maria. 2010. 'Charting Cartographies of Resistance: Lines of Flight in Women Artists' Narratives'. *Gender and Education* 22 (6): 679–96. https://doi.org/10.1080/09540253.2010.519604.
Ulmer, Jasmine B, and Mirka Koro-Ljungberg. 2015. 'Writing Visually through (Methodologocial) Events and Cartography'. *Qualitative Inquiry* 21 (2): 138–52.
Vaillancourt, Régis. 2009. 'I Hear and I Forget, I See and I Remember, I Do and I Understand'. *Canadian Journal of Hospital Pharmacy*, 4, 62 (4): 272–5.
Williams, James. 2008. *Gilles Deleuze's Logic of Sense : A Critical Introduction and Guide*. Edinburgh: Edinburgh University Press. https://www.worldcat.org/title/gilles-deleuzes-logic-of-sense-a-critical-introduction-and-guide/oclc/271179443.
Williams, James. 2011. 'Event'. In *Gilles Deleuze: Key Concepts*, 80–90. Durham: Acumen.
Williams, James. 2013. *Gilles Deleuze's Difference and Repetition: A Critical Introduction and Guide*. Edinburgh: Edinburgh University Press.
Zembylas, Michalinos. 2007. 'Risks and Pleasures: A Deleuzo-Guattarian Pedagogy of Desire in Education'. *British Educational Research Journal* 33 (3): 331–47.
Zembylas, Michalinos. 2018. 'Decolonial Possibilities in South African Higher Education: Reconfiguring Humanising Pedagogies as/with Decolonising Pedagogies'. *South African Journal of Education* 38 (4): 1–9.

Index

actualization 97, 142
   counter-actualize 11, 16, 83, 84, 86, 91, 97–9, 129, 144, 153, 170
affect 7, 11, 14, 15, 22, 42, 58, 59, 66, 72–5, 85, 86, 99, 136, 138, 143, 147, 148, 154, 155
affective becoming 5, 7, 37, 46, 49, 59
affective encounter 54, 72, 75
apartheid 2, 11–13, 21, 36, 41, 42, 44, 88, 91, 147, 175
art 12, 21, 30, 33, 54–7, 62, 73–6, 107, 114, 115, 124, 133, 137, 161, 177
   drawing 8–10, 17, 32, 38, 40, 43–5, 50, 54, 61, 74, 76, 81, 84, 85, 87, 90, 92, 95, 97, 98, 100, 107, 108, 110, 114, 116, 120, 121, 125–7, 131, 142, 161, 170
arts-based inquiry 8, 15, 55–8, 71, 75, 114, 137, 157, 158
assemblage 4–8, 14–17, 23, 2729, 37, 46, 48, 49, 57, 58, 72–5, 84, 91, 97, 98, 102, 120, 123, 124, 141–5, 147, 148, 151, 153, 157, 158
assembled subject 5, 7, 15, 27, 36, 46, 48, 49, 51, 73, 142, 143
autobiography 6, 8, 14, 16, 23, 25, 26, 37, 49, 144, 161

becoming 5–17, 21, 23, 26, 28, 30, 36, 37, 45–7, 49–51, 75, 81–4, 90, 96–103, 107, 108, 110, 111, 115, 116, 119–21, 124, 126, 128, 134, 141–5, 148–51, 153–5, 157–9, 161, 167, 173–5
becoming educator 16, 23, 26, 98, 101, 102, 108, 111, 115, 120, 142, 144
becoming-other 8, 12, 13, 98
Biesta, Gert 54, 55, 72, 110, 111
binary 4, 5, 15–17, 28, 31, 36, 42, 45–47, 49, 50, 59, 98, 100, 142, 143
   educator identity binary 16, 36, 144
   non-binary 5
   personal/professional binary 4

   theory/method binary 8
biography 15, 26, 50, 84, 98, 144
blackness 25, 36–42, 44, 45, 47, 79, 81, 89, 91, 92, 96, 97, 104, 105, 108–110, 112–14, 117, 118, 131, 133, 175, 177
Bloemfontein 1, 19, 36, 39, 86, 91, 93, 119, 132, 134, 145, 147, 175

Cartesian 7, 8, 10, 27, 37, 46, 134, 136
   subject 7, 8, 10, 27, 37, 134, 136
cartography 5, 9, 14–16, 26, 58, 60, 101, 102, 107, 111, 114–16, 119–21, 125–7, 143, 144, 148
collaboration 1, 2, 6, 7, 14, 17, 33, 34, 47, 79, 123, 143, 153, 159, 160, 161
colonize 11, 13, 21, 58, 88, 91
common sense 5, 10, 11, 14, 16, 21, 27, 83, 144, 148, 149, 151, 154, 156
context 1–6, 14, 15, 17, 20–3, 25, 26, 29, 33, 35, 36, 45, 49, 55–9, 61–5, 68, 70, 71, 73, 92, 96, 101, 107, 120, 141–3, 147, 155, 157, 163, 175
continuum 4–7, 14–17, 19, 23, 46, 59, 142–4, 157, 158
COVID-19 2–4, 6, 12, 13, 55, 73, 74, 106, 111, 146, 147, 151, 159, 164, 167, 172
   lockdown 33, 55, 73, 74, 106, 146, 147, 156, 165–7, 170
   pandemic 3, 10, 12, 13, 33, 55, 106, 111, 145, 149, 159, 160, 166, 168
curriculum 2, 13, 22–4

decolonization 2, 5, 6, 8, 12–14, 16, 17, 21–23, 25, 31, 35, 58, 70, 105, 118, 141–4, 157
Deleuze, Gilles 2, 5–8, 10–15, 21, 27–30, 33, 37, 53, 81–4, 86, 94, 97, 99, 101, 102, 107, 115, 124, 141, 143, 144, 148, 149, 151–4, 160, 164, 168, 171, 174
deterritorialize 7
diversity 16, 17, 56, 64, 65, 88, 120
Division of Student Affairs 4, 59

188 Index

educator 9, 2–26, 29–31, 33, 36, 46, 49, 53–5, 57–64, 65, 68–72, 75, 81, 2, 84, 85, 94–6, 99, 101–3, 109–11, 114–16, 119–21, 123, 126, 127, 137, 141–5, 147, 148, 153, 155, 157, 158
educator identity 2, 5–7, 14–17, 26, 31, 36, 46, 49, 57, 59, 121, 143, 144, 147, 148
epistemology 17, 42, 57
equality 11
ethnography 8, 14
event 6–8, 10–13, 15, 16, 25, 41, 54, 58, 81–4, 94, 97, 99, 111, 114, 116, 123–5, 128, 142, 144, 147, 148, 150, 154, 157, 158, 167, 168
experiences 4, 5, 8, 12, 23, 33, 41, 46, 56, 57, 61, 63–6, 71, 80, 82–4, 99, 114, 115, 142, 147, 152, 168, 174, 175

fairness 11
fallist movements
  #FeesMustFall 2, 37, 40, 55, 117, 134, 176
  #RhodesMustFall 2, 4, 37
feedback loop 16, 144
fold, the 5, 23, 107
free State 1, 2, 14, 85, 133, 147, 175, 176

Guattari, Felix 4–8, 14, 21, 28–30, 33, 37, 101, 102, 115, 124, 143, 151, 152

Hickey-Moody, Anna 72–5
hierarchy 4
higher education 2–4, 6–8, 14–17, 21–3, 31, 49, 55, 56, 68, 73, 91, 118, 119, 136, 141–4, 147, 157
human 6, 7, 9, 11, 16, 27, 29, 31, 32, 56, 57, 60, 61, 63, 65, 67, 72, 73, 75, 85, 97, 106, 108, 123–7, 129, 131, 133, 135, 137–9, 144, 147–9
  and non-human 6, 7, 16, 27, 29, 31, 137, 144, 147
  non-human 60, 124, 127

identity 3, 5, 7, 8, 12, 14,–17, 21, 27, 35, 36, 45, 46, 48, 57, 59–61, 81, 82, 86, 98, 105, 106, 108–10, 114, 116, 117, 135, 143, 147–9, 154, 175
  educator identity 2, 5–7, 14–17, 26, 31, 36, 46, 49, 57, 59, 121, 143, 144, 147, 148

Ingold, Tim 17, 101, 120, 125–7

Jansen, Jonathan 22, 23, 104, 110, 176
justice 12, 11, 17, 47, 101, 119

methodology 2, 5–7, 13–15, 17, 19, 21, 26, 28, 29, 32, 48, 49, 58, 69, 84, 101, 142, 143, 145, 148–51
  arts-based inquiry 6, 16, 26, 33, 54–9, 61, 71, 76, 114, 115, 124, 138, 143, 144
  post-qualitative research 27
  qualitative research 8, 26, 27
  workshop 59, 60–2, 64, 67–70, 72, 76, 161
micro-social expression 8
multiplicity 14–16, 28, 37, 46, 49, 58, 99, 102, 107, 123, 124, 129, 143, 144, 147, 149, 159

narrative 1, 2, 5, 6, 8, 13, 15, 19, 21, 23, 26, 30, 32, 33, 36, 37, 39, 41, 42, 45–51, 56, 57, 60, 61, 81, 84, 85, 92–4, 100–3, 106–9, 111, 114–16, 119–21, 123–9, 137, 138, 141–3, 157, 159, 170, 171
network 16, 31, 82, 102, 144, 150

ontology 2, 5, 6, 21, 49, 81, 83, 84
outsider 22

paradox 8, 10, 12–15, 102, 146, 147, 153, 154
pedagogy 4, 13, 22, 24–6, 60, 61, 72, 74, 75, 94, 136, 137
  transformative pedagogy 16, 123, 144
performative
performative narrative 15, 36, 49, 143
performative style 37
performative text 37, 48–51, 143
performative writing 15, 49, 143
photo 17, 159
  snapshot 1, 2, 17, 23, 141, 142
power 6, 7, 8, 12, 13, 17, 22, 24, 42, 62, 64, 65, 70, 72, 114, 115, 125, 129
  hierarchy 22, 41, 64, 65, 70
protest 3, 12, 16, 24, 25, 31, 37, 40, 79, 92, 106, 107, 112, 113, 116–19, 144, 157, 176

reconciliation 11
residence 2, 4, 36–40, 47, 48, 88, 89, 92–4, 99, 105, 106, 112, 113, 134, 165, 167
residence manager 2, 4, 36, 39, 48, 88, 89, 92–4, 99, 105, 112, 134
rhizome 2, 4, 5, 7, 9–11, 14, 15, 17, 28, 31, 32, 59, 74, 85, 101, 102, 108, 120, 141–3, 148, 150, 151, 157, 171

Shimla Park 25, 39, 47, 102, 103, 105, 107, 111–14, 117, 118, 128–30, 132, 134, 145, 147
South Africa 1, 2, 3, 4, 6, 12, 14, 16, 21, 22, 31, 36, 41–43, 48, 49, 55, 56, 74, 79–81, 91, 95, 119, 141, 144, 145, 147, 159, 167, 175, 176, 177
Spinoza, Baruch 147, 152
subjectification 4, 6, 8, 10, 13, 84, 86, 111, 126, 142, 155
subjectivity 1–12, 14–16, 19–24, 26–8, 30–6, 38, 40, 42, 44, 46, 48–50, 53–58, 60–2, 64, 66, 68, 70–2, 74–6, 80–82, 84, 86, 88, 90, 92, 94, 96, 98, 99, 100–4, 106–8, 110, 112, 114, 116, 118–20, 123–6, 128, 130, 132, 134, 136–9, 141–4, 146–8, 150, 152, 154, 156–8, 160, 162, 164, 166, 168, 170, 172, 174
  educator subjectivity 2–10, 12, 14–17, 19–26, 30, 33, 54, 55, 57–59, 62, 63, 70–2, 75, 85, 101, 102, 110, 111, 114, 115, 119, 120, 127, 137, 141–5, 148, 153, 155, 157, 158

territorialize
  deterritorialize 13
thinking habits 4–6, 10, 27, 28
time 2, 6, 8–14, 16, 17, 19, 21, 22, 31 4, 36, 37, 39–41, 43, 46, 48, 49, 51, 53–5, 57–60, 62, 65, 66, 68, 69, 71, 73, 75, 84–90, 92, 95, 96, 97, 99, 101, 107, 108, 110–12, 114, 116, 119, 120, 123, 125–7, 132, 134, 137, 141, 142, 144, 145, 148, 149, 151, 153, 155–7, 159, 164, 166, 167, 169, 171
  Aion 8, 10, 11, 97, 99
  Chronos 8, 10
  future 6, 10–14, 32, 54, 68, 81–4, 86, 91, 95, 97, 99, 107, 112, 120, 123, 125, 126, 130, 137, 138, 142, 145, 147, 148, 150–2, 156, 169
  past 10–13, 24, 25, 31, 32, 36, 37, 42, 54, 79, 82–4, 95, 97, 99, 104, 105, 107, 113, 114, 120, 125, 129, 130, 133, 134, 136, 137, 147, 151
  present 10–13, 15, 32, 36, 37, 51, 54, 55, 79, 82, 84, 86, 90, 97, 99, 101, 107, 108, 114, 120, 125–7, 130, 136–8, 147, 151, 154, 159
time of rapid change 2, 6, 19, 21, 49, 142
transformation 4, 5–8, 12–14, 16, 20–22, 24–6, 31, 36, 41, 46, 49, 57, 61, 65, 67, 70, 80–2, 91, 93, 95, 97–9, 101, 106, 116, 118, 125–7, 141, 142, 144, 146–50, 153, 155–7
  social change 2–6, 8, 11, 12, 14–17, 25, 30, 31, 33, 49, 51, 54, 55, 57–9, 62, 70, 71, 75, 82, 84, 85, 92, 95, 99, 101, 107, 110, 119, 120, 141–5, 147–9, 153, 155–8

vegetal 5

walking 16, 24, 30, 31, 33, 40, 54, 60, 62, 63, 75, 81, 102, 106, 113, 118, 123–6, 128, 129, 131, 132, 134, 136–8, 144, 167, 168, 172
whiteness 9, 15, 23, 35, 36, 38–49, 81, 91, 92, 104–6, 108, 109, 112–14, 118, 143, 175, 176
Williams, James 2, 11, 13, 81–4, 91, 99, 146, 148, 149, 154, 155
wound 8, 81, 98
wound-event 4, 7, 10, 11, 13, 25, 83, 84, 86, 91, 98, 111, 144, 157, 158

Zembylas, Michalinos 22, 24, 25, 61

www.ingramcontent.com/pod-product-compliance
Lightning Source LLC
Chambersburg PA
CBHW061832300426
44115CB00013B/2340